Engraving School Districts With the Cultural Wealth and Social Justice Advocacy of Latina/o/x School Leaders

Engraving School Districts With the Cultural Wealth and Social Justice Advocacy of Latina/o/x School Leaders

Stories From the Field

Kendra Lowery and Silvia Romero-Johnson

LEXINGTON BOOKS

Lanham • Boulder • New York • London

An imprint of The Rowman & Littlefield Publishing Group, Inc.
4501 Forbes Boulevard, Suite 200, Lanham, Maryland 20706
www.rowman.com

86-90 Paul Street, London EC2A 4NE

British Library Cataloguing in Publication Information Available

Library of Congress Cataloging-in-Publication Data

Names: Lowery, Kendra, 1972- author. | Romero-Johnson, Silvia, 1968- author.
Title: Engraving school districts with the cultural wealth and social justice
    advocacy of Latina/o/x school leaders : stories from the field / Kendra Lowery and
    Silvia Romero-Johnson.
Description: Lanham : Lexington Books, [2023] | Includes bibliographical
    references and index.
Identifiers: LCCN 2023002416 (print) | LCCN 2023002417 (ebook) |
    ISBN 9781793615268 (cloth) | ISBN 9781793615275 (epub)
Subjects: LCSH: Educational leadership—United States. | Hispanic Americans—
    Education. | Social justice and education—United States. | Motivation in
    education—United States. | Community and school—United States.
Classification: LCC LB2806 .L68 2023 (print) | LCC LB2806 (ebook) |
    DDC 371.2/011--dc23/eng/20230207
LC record available at https://lccn.loc.gov/2023002416
LC ebook record available at https://lccn.loc.gov/2023002417

Contents

Acknowledgments vii

Introduction 1

1 An Explanation of Constructs and Relevant Research about
Latina/o/x P-12 School Leaders 17

2 Introduction to the School Leaders 35

3 Community Cultural Wealth: Lessons from Childhood, Family,
and Community 41

4 The Pathway to Leadership: Motivations and Steps Taken 55

5 Social Justice Advocacy: Evidence from Latina/o/x School Leaders 63

6 Latino Educational Leadership 77

7 Promising Practices for Engraving Latino Educational Leadership 85

Afterword 91

References 93

Index 101

About the Authors 103

v

Acknowledgments

To the Latina/o/x leaders presented in this book, who dedicate their lives in service to students and families in a multitude of ways. It was an honor to listen, learn, and articulate your lived experiences and leadership practices in this book. Your uncompromised commitment to Latinx families in pursuit of social justice is inspiring, informative, and worthy of exploration by pre-service and existing school leaders, so that we can collectively improve educational outcomes for all students, and Latinx students in particular.

I would like to acknowledge my former colleagues Francisco Martinez, former bilingual resource specialist and current teacher, and in memoriam, Hallie Savage Martinez. They both modeled in profound ways what it means to be a culturally responsive educator. Although they were not formal leaders, they provided a glimpse into the mindset, dispositions, and skills leaders must embrace in order to meaningfully build relationships with and serve Latina/o/x families. Further, they exemplified how leadership transcends formal positions and titles.

I also want to thank Daniel Nerad for supporting my transition to school leadership; Kofi Lomotey for his mentorship and encouragement as I made the transition to higher education; and Jim Scheurich for modeling the type of unrelenting critical analysis of schools and society necessary to dismantle inequities in education.

To the women in my personal, professional, and historical networks who encourage, inspire, and exemplify feminist principles of social justice—thank you.

Thank you to Mom, Wendy, Stacey, and Reggie for your never-ending Christian love, honesty, and grace. Finally, to Robbie—my husband and biggest supporter. You have supported my academic and career pursuits with love, patience, and encouragement.

—Kendra Lowery

To the Latino/a/x leaders who shared their background and professional experiences during the interviews for this book, thank you! You inspire me. Your work matters to the communities in which you serve. Your presence makes it possible for the next generation to be able to see themselves in leadership positions. ¡Gracias!

To the countless colleagues, families, and students I have had the opportunity to co-lead with and serve. To the many mentors I have had over the years as an interpreter, teacher, principal, and central office administrator, you believed in me when I didn't. That helped me persist when the systemic challenges seemed insurmountable. In particular, I would like to acknowledge Dr. Susan Abplanalp, Dr. Jennifer Cheatham, Dr. Brenda Cassellius, and Dr. Dana Monogue who are female superintendents who gave the opportunity to lead. I admire your relentless commitment to excellence and social justice.

Finally, my gratitude to my husband Larien Johnson, without whose support I would not be able to dedicate myself to all the endeavors that are part of my work and passion. To my daughters, Juliana and Gabriela, who are truly my teachers of unconditional love and help me be the better version of myself. To my parents and my grandmother Alcira, who were my role models of what being educated looks like, even when they didn't have the benefit of formal schooling. Your commitment to formal schooling for your children has changed the trajectory of many for generations to come. Lastly, to my granddaughters. You are your ancestors' dreams. I delight in witnessing your love and thirst for learning. May you always thrive!

—Silvia Romero-Johnson

Introduction

School leaders are entrusted with an enormous responsibility. They are entrusted by their communities to ensure that students who attend their schools are provided with safeguards for their mental and physical well-being and have access to high-quality coursework to support their goals, in environments that are welcoming to students and families. Leaders who are equity-minded advocate for and implement policies and practices that support equitable access to and participation in the full range of educational opportunities. They assess progress toward those goals using data disaggregated by identity categories that reveal whether patterns of inequities exist. They take ownership of unmet goals and collaboratively create plans to understand and dismantle sources of inequity. Those plans and goals are inclusive of the voices of the students, families, and community that they serve.

Educators preparing to become leaders may be familiar with standards that identify important skills required to be effective school leaders. These standards commonly include the ability to provide instructional leadership, a clear vision, collaboration and development of positive relationships with families and community, and effective management of financial and human resources.

We use the term "school leader" to refer to those in school administration broadly defined. This includes someone who is a leader of a single building, such as a principal, or someone who leads an entire district in a variety of roles. For example, a district leader could be an associate superintendent, a director of curriculum, or superintendent.

School leaders who incorporate their understanding of the social, political, cultural, and historical contexts of Latina/o/x communities are critical for improving educational experiences and outcomes for Latina/o/x students (Martinez et al., 2020). In particular, Latina/o/x school leaders who draw upon the strengths of their cultural heritage, including their familial and community upbringing, are often well-positioned to contribute to the educational excellence of Latina/o/x students. These strengths are increasingly documented by researchers who study the experiences and characteristics of Latina/o/x school leaders. For example, Hernandez et al. (2014) concluded, "Latina/o leaders who have a conscious understanding of their ethnic identity and incorporate this knowledge into their school leadership practices provide educational insights into the academic needs of Latinas/os" (p. 572). Evidence of this type of leadership includes:

a) leaders who develop equitable relationships with Latina/o/x students;
b) increased parent engagement among Latina/o/x families based on mutual respect and empathy, shared cultural understanding, and a sense of unity;
c) advocacy for bi- or multilingualism in schools that includes Spanish;
d) maintenance of high academic expectations for Latina/o/x students; and
e) the disruption of views among educators and other stakeholders that label Latina/o/x families as inferior.

Latina/o/x school leaders who manifest these characteristics are important to the entire school community. The insights and leadership practices which are characterized by advocacy for equitable school practices and high academic expectations, and are an outgrowth of relationships with students and families, also benefit students and families who do not identify as Latina/o/x.

Unfortunately, despite the strengths Latina/o/x leaders draw on to effectively lead public schools, they are underrepresented in school leadership roles. In 2021, 9.7% of education administrators in the United States identified as Hispanic or Latino (U.S. Department of Labor, 2022). This means that Latina/o/x administrators are vastly underrepresented in comparison to their student counterparts, whose numbers are steadily increasing (Crawford & Fuller, 2017).

Latina/o/x students accounted for the largest increase in percent of students by race in U.S. public P-12 schools between 1970 and 2018. In 1970, Latina/o/x students comprised 5.1% of public school students, compared to 25.4% in 2013 (Orfield et al., 2016). In the fall of 2020, Latina/o/x students comprised 28% of the public school student population (National Center for Education Statistics, 2022b).

While Latina/o/x students currently constitute 28% of the public school student population, Latina/o/x administrators constitute 9.7% of education administrators.

Table I.1   Latinx Students as a Percentage of the U.S. Public School Population, 1970–2020 (National Center for Educational Statistics, 2022b; Orfield et al., 2016)

Year	1970	2020
%	5.1	28

THE URGENT NEED FOR LATINA/O/X SCHOOL LEADERS

It is critically important that schools identify institutional approaches (strategies school systems develop through policies and practices) to meet the needs of Latina/o/x students and families. The urgency for such approaches, which should include hiring more Latina/o/x administrators, is evident when considering the ways in which many Latina/o/x students and families are currently being underserved in schools across the United States.

Data regarding the academic achievement of Latina/o/x students illustrate that schools present barriers to positive experiences and outcomes despite the resiliency and value of education among Latina/o/x families (Hayes et al., 2015; Vega et al., 2015). For example, Ceja (2004) discovered that parents found "their own ways of instilling in their children the importance of doing well in school and going to college" (p. 345). However, institutional practices often create barriers to success. For example, monolingual instructional practices support English-only, privilege English, and devalue Spanish speakers, even those who are learning English. These policies and practices often lead to segregated classrooms, based on the assumption that children whose home language is Spanish and are not fluent in English do not have the skills or abilities to access rigorous curriculum (Gándara & Aldana, 2014).

Although the dropout rate for Latina/o/x students drastically decreased from 15.1% in 2010 to 7.4% in 2020, the 2020 dropout rate was higher than the rate for students who identify as two or more races (6.5%), White (4.8%), Black (4.2%), and Asian (2.4%) students, as well as the overall dropout rate (5.3%) (National Center for Education Statistics, 2022c).

Further, 2018–2019 graduation data reveal 82% of Latina/o/x students who attended public high schools graduated within four years of starting ninth grade (the adjusted cohort graduation rate), compared to 93% of Asian/Pacific Islander students, of White students, 86% of students overall, 80% of Black students, and 74% of American Indian/Alaska Native students (National Center for Education Statistics, 2021a).

Crawford and Fuller (2017) posited "one potential cause of Latino student underperformance is the underrepresentation of Latino school leaders . . . research suggests that school leaders who understand the cultural background and lived experiences of students tend to be more effective in improving

Table I.2 Dropout Rate (%) for 16- to 24-Year-Olds by Race/Ethnicity: 2010–2020 (National Center for Educational Statistics, 2022c)

Race/Ethnicity	2010	2020
Overall	7.4	5.3
American Indian/Alaska Native	12.4	11.5
Hispanic*	15.1	7.4
Two or more races	5.4	6.5
White	5.1	4.8
Black	8.0	4.2
Asian	4.1	2.4

*Term used to denote Latina/o/x students by the NCES.

Table I.3 Adjusted Cohort Graduation Rate (%) for Public School Students, by Race (National Center for Educational Statistics, 2021a)

Total	American Indian/ Alaska Native	Black	Hispanic	White	Asian/Pacific Islander
86	74	80	82	89	93

outcomes" (p. 1167). Although being Latina/o/x does not mean one is automatically capable of meeting the needs of Latina/o/x students, it is likely that Latina/o/x administrators who lead from an equity-oriented perspective have assets based on their identities and experiences. These assets should be considered when hiring for administrative positions, particularly in districts where Latina/o/x students are a large or growing population (Rodela & Rodríguez-Mojica, 2019; Santamaría et al., 2014).

Leadership development is also important, particularly as a way to address the root causes of education inequities such as underrepresentation of Latina/o/x administrators and underperformance of Latina/o/x students. Therefore, a top priority for educational leadership preparation programs in higher education and school districts should be the development of "leaders across the educational pipeline that have the capacity to promote cultural, linguistic, and historical connections for Latino communities" (Rodríguez et al., 2016, p. 148).

> A top priority for educational leadership preparation programs in higher education, and school districts should be the development of "leaders across the educational pipeline that have the capacity to promote cultural, linguistic, and historical connections for Latino communities. (Rodríguez et al., 2016, p. 148)

Latina/o/x school leaders who reflect upon their lived experiences within their unique sociocultural contexts and incorporate their cultural strengths into their leadership practice have much to offer school districts and communities in general, and Latina/o/x students and families in particular. School leaders and educational leadership preparation program faculty can learn from these experiences to understand and explore how administrators' culturally responsive practices are and can be engraved upon school districts. We use the term "engraved" to mean evidence that leadership practicwes of Latina/o/x school leaders that facilitate increased access and equity for Latina/o/x students and families have created lasting changes within schools.

PURPOSE OF THIS BOOK

The purpose of this book is to share the lived experiences of Latina/o/x school leaders that inform their approach to school leadership. We share these experiences through the lens of different strengths, capital, or wealth, collectively referred to as "community cultural wealth," a phrase coined by Yosso (2005). These different forms of cultural wealth identify multiple ways of knowing among traditionally marginalized/underserved/mistreated groups. Largely because the voices and experiences of traditionally marginalized groups have not been centered in decision-making in schools and society, their ways of knowing are often unrecognized. By bringing these ways of knowing to the forefront of Latina/o/x school leadership in this book, we highlight the ways in which these leaders contribute to Latino Educational Leadership, a form of social justice and culturally responsive school leadership that centers Latino cultures and experiences (Rodríguez et al., 2016; 2018).

The terms "community cultural wealth" and "culturally responsive school leadership" will be described in the next chapter. Next, we will explain the difference between asset- and deficit-based thinking since they are central to understanding why the leadership we describe is essential for educational equity.

DEFICIT- VS. ASSET-BASED THINKING

It is important to understand the fundamental differences between asset- and deficit-based thinking. Asset-based or strengths-based thinking directly challenges all-too-common approaches to thinking about groups of people who underperform based on traditionally held standards or norms, as the problem. Deficit-based thinking occurs when members of a group are considered the problem because of a deficiency or deficiencies, which are attributed to the group. As a result, they are blamed for the inequities they face. For example, in our roles as educators, we have witnessed countless conversations where

Black and Brown families were blamed for underperformance in achievement categories, such as graduation rates or academic proficiency. Similar conversations took place regarding overrepresentation in negative outcomes such as suspension or expulsion rates. Seemingly well-intentioned people would simultaneously blame "families who just don't value education" and self-identify as social justice advocates. This type of thinking which blames students and families for systemic inequities is often referred to as deficit-based, deficit-laden, or deficit thinking.

As Valencia (2010) summarized, the deficit thinking model as it relates to schools, rests on the belief "that the student who fails in school does so because of his/her internal deficits or deficiencies" (pp. 6–7). For example, Alemán (2009) unpacked the deficit beliefs spoken by a Utah government official in 2005. The official juxtaposed students in majority White schools, who grow up with "a lot of exposure to vocabulary and reading," with students in majority Latina/o schools who "don't have much exposure to vocabulary" before school. Alemán explained that the statement revealed the official's assumptions that students attending predominantly Latina/o schools are less skilled and have less vocabulary as they enter school. Alemán concluded that the rhetoric and underlying assumptions were "indicative of wider attempts to assign blame to those with less institutional power and to devalue the cultural and community assets that are present in communities of color" (p. 295).

In contrast, some school leaders take a critical approach to understanding inequities which supports asset-based thinking. They believe it is the responsibility of societal institutions —not the responsibility of individual students and families who are treated inequitably—such as school districts, to end systems of oppression. Leaders who take a critical perspective acknowledge that many of these systems of oppression were created before any of us were born. However, they believe that while we do not have to bear guilt for oppressive systems and actions that we did not create, we must continuously be vigilant about examining those systems and how we may or may not contribute to them, in order to eliminate inequities.

Instead of blaming families for the inequities they face, school leaders who have a critical perspective recognize that families have strengths, or assets, that should be acknowledged and incorporated into school practices. This approach does not assume that any group is inferior or more problematic than others. Therefore, differences in experiences and outcomes are attributed to systemic factors such as oppression, inequitable treatment, or lack of understanding about different cultural norms and experiences. Further, those who promote asset-based thinking seek to understand individual and cultural attributes (or strengths) that promote their positive development, thriving, and resilience, even in the face of systemic oppression. The differences between deficit- and asset-based thinking about students and families are summarized in table 4. The table reveals key points about each type of thinking that are in direct opposition to each other. Overall, the major attribute of deficit-based thinking is blaming families for their perceived faults. The major attribute of asset-based thinking is valuing the strengths families bring while critiquing institutions to address inequities.

Table I.4   Differences between Deficit- and Asset-Based Thinking about Students and Families

Deficit-Based Thinking	*Asset-Based Thinking*
Blames students and families for inequitable educational outcomes	Blames institutions for inequitable educational outcomes
Believes some communities have negative cultural and familial traits that impede academic success	Believes every community has value and identifies strengths that contribute to academic success
Sees "struggle" as primarily within students and families who are "at risk" of failure	Sees "struggle" as primarily within institutions which are unable to effectively reach all students and families
Focuses on what families need to change in order to achieve equity	Focuses on what school institutions need to change in order to achieve equity
Thinks in broad strokes about groups without developing relationships to understand individuals	Understands general group characteristics in conjunction with knowledge of individuals developed through trusting relationships
If advocates *for* families, does so with the assumption that families are incompetent and need a "savior"	Advocates *with* families by centering their voices and multiple forms of expertise, including lived experience
Focuses on what students and families cannot do	Focuses on what students and families can do
Holds low expectations for academic success and family engagement	Holds high expectations for academic success and family engagement
Attributes lack of representation in rigorous classes and experiences to lack of student ability	Attributes lack of representation in rigorous classes and experiences to institutional lack of access and opportunity
Limits students' potential	Unlocks students' potential
Does not engage in self-reflection about underlying assumptions	Engages in self-reflection about personal assumptions and societal factors that contribute to inequity

*We developed this in part, with content from Renkly and Bertolini (2013), Lombardi (2016), Ormand (2019), and Valencia (2010).

Review the differences between deficit- and asset-based thinking in table I.4.
Reflection Questions:

1. In what ways, if any, have you engaged in deficit-based thinking about students and families? What about Latina/o/x students and families in particular?
2. What knowledge and reflection do you need to engage in to shift to asset-based thinking?
3. Have you witnessed deficit thinking expressed either verbally or manifested in policies and practices regarding students and families among your colleagues? What about Latina/o/x students and families in particular?
4. What strategies might you use to disrupt deficit thinking and practices among your colleagues?

Leadership that is informed by cultural wealth directly challenges the viewing of Latina/o/x families from deficit perspectives in two ways. First, leaders are able to articulate those aspects of cultural wealth they experienced in their own lives. Second, their understanding of different forms of cultural wealth due to their lived experience positions them to identify and value the cultural wealth within other families. This, in turn, makes it more likely they will be able to challenge deficit notions of Latina/o/x families. Therefore, our exploration of Latina/o/x school leaders is an asset-based, rather than deficit-based examination of the educational experiences of Latina/o/x students, families, and administrators.

We explore the lived experiences and school leadership practices of eight public school leaders across the United States to demonstrate how leaders draw upon their community cultural wealth from childhood through their careers, to engage in social justice advocacy. We also demonstrate how certain practices and values of the leaders have been engraved upon their school districts as they influenced norms, culture, and policy.

WHY THIS BOOK IS IMPORTANT

A few existing books explore the assets and leadership styles of Latina/o/x administrators (Martinez & Méndez-Morse, 2021; Rodriguez et al., 2018). These texts underscore the argument that the hiring and support of Latina/o/x administrators benefits school communities, and is particularly beneficial for the success of Latina/o/x students and families. In addition to underscoring this, our book is unique because it emphasizes the ways in which Latina/o/x administrators make enduring changes in schools and districts. This important point invites conversation about the necessity of school districts to foster culturally responsive leadership within all leaders. Therefore, the responsibility for creating equitable engagement and achievement for Latina/o/x students and families will not rest solely upon Latina/o/x administrators. Accordingly, while their assets are unique to their race, ethnicity, heritage, and culture, the ways Latina/o/x administrators acknowledge, value, and respond to Latina/o/x families can inform leadership practices.

Exploration of Latina/o/x educational leaders across the pipeline from preschool to college is of increasing interest (Hernandez et al., 2014; Lowery & Romero-Johnson, 2018; Rodela & Rodriguez-Mojica, 2019). A focus on Latina/o/x leadership is necessary because while Latina/o/x students have general experiences and needs similar to other students, they also face specific challenges due to insufficient practices and policies to address diverse Latinx identities, languages, and cultures in American schools (Galindo, 2021). This does not mean that Latina/o/x administrators bear the sole responsibility to educate Latinx students (González, 2010). Rather, we hope increased understanding of the assets of Latina/o/x administrators will (a) shed light on why Latina/o/x leaders are essential and (b) inform efforts to increase recruitment, retention, and promotion of Latina/o/x administrators who shape district practices to improve conditions for Latina/o/x students and families.

Our exploration of Latina/o/x leadership styles that promote educational opportunity, equity, and excellence also can inform the leadership practices of non-Latinx school leaders who choose to dismantle (tear down, or end) oppressive practices in schools. To review, examples of oppressive practices that should be dismantled include:

- deficit thinking which leads to low academic expectations;
- upholding a monolingual school culture by privileging English and not valuing home languages other than English; and
- denying access to rigorous academics due to an erroneous association between limited English proficiency and limited cognitive development.

Non-Latina/o/x administrators who agree to learn from Latina/o/x administrators who model uplifting the cultural assets of families and dismantling oppressive practices have the opportunity to reproduce or engrave anti-oppressive practices in their practice and district. This engraving ensures that these practices are sustainable beyond one or two leaders, to the benefit of all stakeholders.

Our analysis of cultural wealth challenges deficit thinking about Latina/o/x educational stakeholders which focuses on what Latina/o/x administrators, students, and families lack (Kemp-Graham, 2015; McCarther et al., 2012). In contrast, leaders who exhibit cultural wealth and social justice challenge deficit notions of Latina/o/x students as underachievers. Leaders advocate for students by:

- focusing on how schools have underserved them;
- reallocating resources;
- changing inequitable institutional structures; and
- facilitating equitable family collaboration (Cambron-McCabe & McCarthy, 2005; DeMatthews et al., 2016; Santamaria, 2014).

POSITIONALITY

Next, we explain how we came to know each other and how our own lived experiences informed our motivations and approach to the content presented in this book. This process is called reflecting on our positionality. Jacobson and Mustafa (2021) describe positionality as the combination of our social identities, which "include but are not limited to class, citizenship, ability, age, race, sexual orientation, cis/trans status, and gender [that] affect the way we see and interpret the world around us" (pp. 1–2). As researchers, we acknowledge this and do not see ourselves as entirely neutral or uninfluenced by our experiences. Therefore, as Jacobson and Mustafa point out, we agree that "it is important to highlight researchers' motivations for conducting research and how one's background and experiences impact this motivation" (p. 2).

Factors such as the changing nature of our identities and uncertainty about which aspects of our identities are most influential to our perspectives add to the complexities of positionality. We offer a brief explanation of our positionality as an introduction so that readers get a glimpse of our personal and professional backgrounds, how we connect to the topic of Latina/o/x school leadership, and our relation to the experiences of the school leaders we interviewed.

We came to know each other through our work in the same school district several years ago. We worked more directly together as administrators. We have previously collaborated on a manuscript and conference presentation on Latinx school leadership. We both have doctoral degrees in education. Our research training and experiences, although different, prepared us to collect and analyze the school leaders' experiences and present them in a meaningful and engaging way. Silvia's lived experience as a Latina school administrator and as a colleague with many of the school leaders in the book, uniquely situates her to examine these stories from an insider perspective.

SILVIA

My first job in education was in my native country of Argentina, where I was hired to be an English as Foreign Language teacher for first and second graders in a public school. The country had recognized that being fluent in a language other than one's home language could provide an advantage to students. Public schools wanted to remain competitive and relevant, as many parents were selecting to enroll their children in private schools where the design of the schooling experience included universal access to instruction in English as a Foreign Language.

After immigrating to the United States, it was clear to me that my bilingualism would be an asset, so I applied and became an interpreter for Spanish-speaking families in a mid-size urban school district. Once the coordinator of the program realized I had been a teacher, she encouraged me to enroll in a teacher preparation program. I became a bilingual mathematics teacher, as a support teacher and a classroom teacher, a teacher leader, a principal, and a central office administrator.

The district where I was working at the time was experiencing rapid growth in the enrollment of students who speak Spanish at home. One of my duties as a central office coordinator for bilingual and dual language programs was to support principals and their leadership teams to go through the experience of transforming their schools to be ready to welcome students in dual language programs. My job went beyond the implementation of programs. It really was about leading a change process of redesigning schools to move beyond the current status-quo they were in at the time of implementation to a new way of doing schooling from an asset-based perspective. I met Kendra during this time and I appreciated her openness to learn and to go beyond what was comfortable. It isn't always easy for monolingual administrators to lead this change but being monolingual does not preclude one from being an effective advocate.

KENDRA

My first job as a public school educator was as a Minority Services Counselor (an Equity Officer in today's lexicon) whose function was to support the academic achievement of students of color in a high school. I spent many years as a classroom teacher, then district-wide professional development teacher before I became an assistant principal of a middle school and assumed leadership of its dual language immersion (DLI) program. I knew Silvia prior to becoming an administrator but built a stronger relationship with her during this time, as she was the districtwide administrator for global languages.

I am monolingual and therefore quickly became aware that my monolingualism was a barrier to developing relationships with students and families who spoke Spanish. The presence of a Spanish-language interpreter created distance between me and Spanish-speaking families. It makes sense—the interpreter became the trusted school personnel because they could communicate directly and understand the student and caregiver. That, coupled with my position as a school administrator which often represented power with the potential to deny access, from the family's perspective, made it clear to me why bilingual administrators in a bilingual school are essential. Although I am no longer in that role, the experience combined with working on this book and reading scholarship by bilingual Latinx scholars who incorporate Spanish language into their writing, propelled me to learn Spanish. By learning Spanish, I am opening up possibilities for increased communication and interactions with Spanish speakers, which, in turn, creates opportunities for mutual understanding and respect. I am an emerging self-taught Spanish speaker, which by no means makes me an expert on the language or culture; rather, it better positions me to be a learner about the rich, diverse histories and cultures of Latina/o/x peoples.

I have been committed to educational equity and inclusive education with a focus on anti-racism and Black students throughout my career. Leading a dual language immersion program deepened my understanding of educational equity for Latina/o/x students, in particular. While I believed universal principles of equity, opportunity, and educational access are important for all students, I deepened my understanding about the importance of learning particular historic and contemporary contexts that situate individual lived experiences of the Latina/o/x families and students that I served. I am currently an associate dean and associate professor in an educational leadership program at a midwestern university, where I research social justice leadership and race. I also facilitate university-school partnerships focused on increasing academic achievement for historically underserved and racially and linguistically diverse students.

Preferred Use of Terms

Ethnoracial labels are terms used to describe a person's ethnicity and race. The origins of these terms are embedded in social, political, and historical contexts of society and often represent tensions between government or institutions who create ethnoracial labels for groups (i.e. U.S. Census) and the agency of groups or individuals to identify themselves. Ideally, each person should select the label that best describes their identity as they currently view it. Ethnoracial labels may change over time as social, political, and historical contexts and users' identities evolve. Some individuals or groups may completely reject labels created by the government. For example, some Indigenous people do not identify with any of the labels used in the United States.

We raise these points because many terms are used to identify people of Latina/o/x descent. For example, the term "Hispanic" is typically used to denote an ethnic, not a racial category. However, the U.S. government, other institutions, and individuals including those who identify as Hispanic might use them interchangeably.

Ethnoracial labels are socially created and, therefore, must not be seen as terms that describe a monolithic group. This is certainly the case with the terms "Hispanic," "Latino," or "Latinx." Cecilia, one of the school leaders we interviewed, captured this when she reflected upon her experience in a national organization for aspiring Latinx administrators. She said,

> That's why I loved being part of the cohort, because even being Hispanic, we're not all the same. We may be grouped into one big group. . . . But the Mexicans, from the Cubans from the people from Colombia, we are all very, very different and we all bring different perspectives. So again, when I was in the group, I loved that because there were two or three of us that were Cuban, but many of them were either Mexican, Peruvian. So it's just so great to listen to the other cultures different than my own.

Mora et al. (2022) traced the history of the term "Latinx." The term seems to have first emerged around 2005 and gained popularity by 2015. The year 2019 marked the first time the term "Latinx" was used nationally on an English-language broadcast when Jorge Ramos, a U.S. Latino media host, used the term in a Democratic primary debate. The use of an "x" in "Latinx" denotes a shift away from an "o" in the widely used term "Latino" which "symbolized a highly gendered, male, and thus non-inclusive vision of Latinidad" (p. 1171). Ramos's use of the term "Latinx" sparked controversy by those who asserted it is not a direct translation of a Spanish word; it is inappropriate to use non-gendered language in a language that is gendered; and it is not being used by large numbers of Latinos beyond elite, academic spaces. The controversy reignited long-standing questions about identity, power, the politics of self-definition, and the state's role in ethnoracial labeling, gender, and language.

A survey of U.S.-born Latino Californians revealed that the term "Latinx" is more popular than some previously thought (Mora et al., 2022). Education status was not associated with the use of the term; however, lower income Latinos reported using the term more frequently than high income Latinos. Perhaps, most interesting, "individuals who identify as 'Latinx' also identify as 'Hispanic' and 'Latino'" (p. 1187), suggesting that the terms may be used interchangeably or in different contexts by the same person.

We concur with Rodríguez et al. (2018) who recognized that while "the term Latinx has gained traction and been embraced by some academics as a more gender inclusive term that pushes against a binary application of

Latina/o . . . there are others that prefer Latina/o or even Latino for various reasons" (p. 2). Like these authors, we did not want to only use Latinx since it is currently on trend. At the same time, we recognize that a belief that the term is merely a trend may be problematic. Vidal-Ortiz and Martínez (2018) see use of the term "as a continuity of internal shifting group dynamics and disciplinary debates" (p. 384). Adding to this complexity is Mora et al.'s (2022) important observation that

> what is clear is that "Latinx" identifiers exhibit patterns that ethnic studies and other culture scholars have long identified—namely that individuals build a cultural repertoire of labels and group definitions and that they can switch between labels depending on the context at hand. (p. 1188)

We heeded Mora et al.'s recommendation to avoid using labels such as "Latino" or "Latinx" as "mutually exclusive or either/or" (p. 1188). Accordingly, our choices regarding which term to use were informed by research that frames our explanations and analyses, as well as the preferences of the school leaders we interviewed.

Since our readers will most likely be English speakers and all of our interviewees are public education school leaders in the United States, we generally use Latina/o/x to be the most inclusive of preferred terms. We also use Hispanic, Latina, Latino, and Latinx depending on the context of the research we draw upon, as stated earlier. We deferred to the school leaders' preferred terms for self-identification and discussion of their cultural group. To summarize, when different labels are used, they represent the preferred language of the speaker or researcher.

Finally, as way of introduction, we summarize each chapter to provide a brief overview of the book. Chapter 1 presents an overview of concepts that will be explored in the book along with what researchers have uncovered about Latina/o/x school leaders related to these concepts. We explain the origins, development, and applications of the concept of community cultural wealth and other key concepts such as critical race counterstories, *testimonios*, and social justice leadership. We also introduce the concept of engraving leadership and how we apply it throughout the book. Chapter 2 includes our methods for collecting and analyzing our interview data. We also introduce our interview participants, who we will refer to as school leaders. We use pseudonyms to identify all of the school leaders. Chapter 3 presents school leaders' reflections regarding community cultural wealth that informed their leadership practices. In chapter 4, we offer our analysis of how leaders described what motivated them to pursue formal leadership roles and the steps they took to achieve their goals. In chapter 5, we present a range of social justice advocacy practices the leaders engage in on behalf of Latinx students and families. The leaders discuss how their practices positively influenced Latinx student and family engagement, and achievement. In chapter 6, we revisit the concept of Latino Educational Leadership in relation to our discussion of the Latina/o/x school leaders' actions, reflections, and experiences. Finally, in chapter 7 we identify mindsets, skills, and opportunities needed for school/district leaders to recruit, hire, retain, and include Latina/o/x school leaders in organizational decision-making in significant and enduring ways. The chapter ends with an explanation of how certain mindsets and practices of Latina/o/x administrators can be sustained by non-Latina/o/x leaders.

Chapter 1

An Explanation of Constructs and Relevant Research about Latina/o/x P-12 School Leaders

This chapter serves two purposes. One purpose is to explain several constructs that we use to explore the lived experiences of the Latina/o/x school leaders presented in this book. We present Latina/o/x school leaders' experiences within the concept of community cultural wealth (Yosso, 2005). This concept, or construct, is rooted in critical race theory (CRT), a complex theory with a rich tradition of scholarship. Therefore, we provide an overview of critical race theory, followed by an explanation of Latino critical race theory, often referred to as LatCrit. Then, we explain critical race counterstories since we present counterstories of Latina/o/x school leaders in this book. We explain community cultural wealth, particularly as it relates to Latinx students, families, and educators, followed by constructs relevant to Latino school leadership. We delineate how critical race theory is the foundation for LatCrit, and trace connections between CRT, community cultural wealth, and social justice leadership, advocacy, culturally responsive leadership, and Latino Educational Leadership.

Our second purpose is to highlight research that already exists about Latina/o/x school leaders. The research will provide context for making meaning about similarities and differences between existing research and the experiences of the school leaders in this book. Since the early 2000s, increasing studies examine the role of identity among Latina/o/x school administrators and the extent to which identity is a contributing factor to social justice leadership practices. Of note, many of these studies utilize CRT/LatCrit as a theoretical framework and/or methodology to understand Latino administrators' experiences (e.g., Hernandez & Murakami, 2016b; Martinez et al., 2016, 2020; Rodela & Rodriguez-Mojica, 2020). We share some of this scholarship to increase awareness about the way Latina/o/x school leaders are being centered in research, and to inspire more research in this area. We also connect research findings to the constructs mentioned above. To do this, we embed our understanding of the research into the relevant sections. Next, we explain critical race theory.

CRITICAL RACE THEORY

Critical race theory (CRT) originated from legal scholars who challenged the absence of race and racism in legal analysis (Yosso et al., 2001). These scholars sought to understand the law's "role in the construction and maintenance of social domination and subordination" (West, 1995, p. xi). In other words, critical race theorists explore how existing legal paradigms uphold White supremacy by uncovering "the ongoing dynamics of racialized power, and its embeddedness in practices and values" even when those practices and values no longer appear to perpetuate "explicit, formal manifestations of racism" (Crenshaw et al., 1995, p. xxix). While some people argue that current U.S. laws are race neutral because they do not explicitly deny certain races access and opportunities, CRT theorists reject notions of race neutrality.

Critical race theorists and activists are "engaged in studying and transforming the relationship among race, racism, and power" (Delgado & Stefancic, 2017, p. 3). CRT is distinct from traditional civil rights theories and actions because it "questions the very foundations of the liberal order, including equality theory, legal reasoning, Enlightenment rationalism, and neutral principles of constitutional law" (p. 3). Ladson-Billings (2021) articulated an important distinction between critical race theorists and other theorists that study the meanings, experiences, and impact of race in society. She noted CRT scholars believe "that racism is not some random, isolated act of individuals behaving badly. Rather, to a CRT scholar racism is the normal order of things in US society" (p. 37).

Critical race theory is grounded in the works of scholars such as Karl Marx, Antonio Gramsci, and Paulo Friere; Black and Chicano scholars and activists such as W. E. B. DuBois, Sojourner Truth, and Cesar Chavez (Delgado & Stefancic, 2017); and feminist standpoint theories such as Black feminist thought (Collins, 1990). Preeminent scholars who contributed to the development of critical race theory include (but certainly are not limited to) Derrick Bell (1980), Kimberlé Crenshaw (1991), Richard Delgado (1984), Alan Freeman (1978), Angela Harris (1994), and Patricia Williams (1991).

Fundamentally, CRT scholars seek to uncover and reject White supremacy by centering the voices and experiences of historically marginalized racial groups (often referred to as people of color) through research and analysis. Related to our earlier discussion of deficit-thinking, Yosso (2005) explained that analysis "through a CRT lens means critiquing deficit theorizing and data that may be limited by its omission of the voices of People of Color" (p. 75).

Ladson-Billings and Tate (1995) bridged CRT to education in the United States in their seminal work "Toward a Critical Race Theory of Education." They explained that critical race theorists in education "theorize race and use it as an analytic tool for understanding school inequity" (p. 48). There are not strict tenets or principles to which critical race theorists in education must adhere. However, common tenets of CRT pedagogy and research include a belief in:

- the permanence of race and racism in society;
- the intersectionality of race and racism with other forms of oppression;
- challenges to traditional, dominant claims of meritocracy and colorblindness that mask power inequities;
- the centrality of experiential knowledge and voices of people of color;
- a commitment to anti-racism, anti-oppression in all of its forms, and social justice; and
- the utilization of interdisciplinary approaches to understand how racism and other forms of oppression influence experience (Bernal, 2002; Ladson-Billings & Tate, 1995; Solórzano, 1998; Yosso et al., 2001).

CRT has evolved since its creation. Theorists have developed subsets of critical race theories particular to unique racial and other historically marginalized identities. Examples include AsianCrit, which centers the experiences and voices of Asian Americans (Iftikar & Museus, 2019), and TribalCrit, which directly addresses the issues Indigenous peoples face in the United States (Brayboy, 2006).

In addition to focusing attention on the unique experiences of different racial groups, these theories help stretch thinking about racial issues beyond a Black/White binary. Increasing scholarship centers the lived experiences of Latinx peoples through the lens of Latino critical race theory (LatCrit). LatCrit informed our approach to understanding the stories of the Latina/o/ox school leaders presented in this book, so we will provide background on LatCrit in the next section.

Latino Critical Race Theory (LatCrit)

Latino critical race theory, or LatCrit, is important for our analysis of Latinx administrators because it extends critical race theory to an examination of race and the effects of racism among Latinx peoples (Hernandez et al., 2014). The theory is concerned with a "coalitional Latina/Latino pan-ethnicity" (Solórzano & Bernal, 2001, p. 311). As with CRT, LatCrit emerged from critiques of Eurocentric foundations within legal studies. LatCrit theorists view

LatCrit theory, community and praxis as an effort, both to interject "Latinas/os" into the ongoing development of critical approaches to law and policy, as well as to expand and advance the growing field of critical outsider jurisprudence initiated in previous years by [their] predecessors. (p. 170)

Bernal (2002) offered a distinction between LatCrit and CRT and explained why LatCrit is more useful as a tool to examine Chicanao students' lives. She noted that while LatCrit is similar to CRT, it "addresses issues often ignored by critical race theorists" and adds "important dimensions to a critical race analysis . . . such as language, immigration, ethnicity, culture, identity, phenotype, and sexuality." In sum, "LatCrit is a theory that elucidates Latinas/Latinos' multidimensional identities and can address the intersectionality of racism, sexism, classism, and other forms of oppression" (p. 108). Additionally, Davila and Aviles de Bradley (2010) explained, LatCrit offers, "a context for the social, historical, and political reception and impact of Latina/os in the U.S., and provides theoretical space to analyze experiences of language and immigration among other lived experiences rooted in the resistance and oppression of Latinas/os" (p. 40).

Solórzano's (1998) study of Chicano and Chicana graduate students is one of the earliest applications of LatCrit to education. Students experienced microaggressions, or subtle, covert forms of racism and sexism by being made to feel out of place in the academy, having lower academic expectations communicated to them by their professors, and racist and sexist attitudes and comments. The responses shared by participants in the study reveal why centering their voices is important for shedding light on the ways individuals and institutions create oppressive environments and marginalize students.

Bernal (2002) also studied the lived experiences of Chicanao college students in an early application of LatCrit to education. Through a comparison of Chicanao college students' experiences from a Eurocentric and a LatCrit perspective, Bernal (2002) demonstrated how LatCrit is an appropriate exploration of Chicanao students' experience because they have unique experiences in education which should be explored through a critical raced-gender epistemological (ways of knowing) lens that understands and centers their perspectives. She found that different perspectives held "vastly different views of what counts as knowledge, specifically regarding language, culture, and community commitment" (pp. 120–121).

Other examples of LatCrit in education outside of educational leadership (which will be discussed in the next chapter) include Davila and Aviles de Bradley (2010) whose CRT and LatCrit analysis of data about Latinas/os within the Chicago Public Schools revealed systemic inequities; a conceptualization of four different types of microaffirmations that was developed after listening to African American, Latinx, and mixed race college students (Rolón-Dow & Davison, 2020), and an analysis of data from a Texas high school which revealed racial injustice meted out against Latinas/os in school relationships, policies, and practices (Cooper Stein et al., 2018).

In accordance with LatCrit, we maintain that neither the underrepresentation of Latina/o/x school leaders nor the underachievement of Latina/o/x students as evidenced by data such as test scores is not due to deficits on their part. Rather these outcomes are due to shortcomings within educational systems that are supposed to engaged in equitable hiring and educational practices (Bernal, 2002; Rodríguez et al., 2016; Yosso, 2005). To understand the lived experiences of Latinas/os in schools, CRT scholars and LatCrit scholars are often guided by the CRT tenet of centering the voices of Latinos through counterstorytelling and *testimonios*.

CRITICAL RACE COUNTERSTORIES (COUNTERNARRATIVES)

Solórzano and Yosso's (2000) chapter, "Toward a Critical Race Theory of Chicana and Chicano Education" is an analysis of schooling experiences unique to people of Chicana/o heritages. This is particularly important because CRT theorists maintain that racism creates a narrative through storytelling that upholds White dominance and privilege. Further, Solórzano and Yosso (2002) maintained, "[u]nacknowledged White privilege helps maintain racism's stories" (p. 27). CRT and LatCrit directly challenge this racism because a central tenet of these theories is the centering of voices who have been previously silenced or marginalized (i.e., Latinaos). Counter-storytelling has emerged as both a tenet of CRT/LatCrit and a research methodology which can yield insight into the existence of racism and the ways people of color have experienced and resisted against it.

Counter-storytelling as a methodology in LatCrit highlights the experiential knowledge of Latinaos, while allowing for the analysis and recognition of nuances within groups, thereby challenging monolithic assumptions about entire groups (Delgado & Stefancic, 2017). This method also sheds light on "the experiences of people of color that produce distinctive knowledge to counter deficit storytelling" (Rolón-Dow & Davison, 2020, p. 4). Delgado (1988) argued that counter-storytelling is important because it allows for the telling of stories by people typically on the margins of society. Their stories "can shatter complacency and challenge the status quo" (p. 2414), "quicken and engage conscience" and "stir imagination in ways in which more conventional discourse cannot" (p. 2415).

In an explanation of how counter-storytelling can be used as a framework for education research, Solórzano and Yosso (2002) defined the counterstory as a "method of telling the stories of those people whose experiences are often not told" which can be used as "a tool for exposing, analyzing, and challenging the majoritarian stories of racial privilege" and "can help strengthen traditions of social, political, and cultural survival and resistance." (p. 32)

There are three general types of counterstories: first-person testimonios, other people's narratives written in the third person, and stories based on multiple data sources which are combined to create composite characters (see Solórzano & Yosso, 2002 for references to examples of each of these types). In this book, we present the counterstories of Latina/o/x school leaders mainly as *testimonios* and sometimes write about the leaders in the third person.

First-person counterstories are personal stories or narratives which are autobiographical in nature and include a CRT analysis of the author's experiences. These narratives are often referred to as *testimonios* when contextualized within LatCrit. DeNicolo et al. (2015) defined *testimonios* as "counternarratives of . . . individual and collective experiences" (p. 230). *Testimonios* can reveal unique experiences about the intersections of multiple identities such as race and gender. Martinez et al. (2020) offered a gendered analysis of the experiences of Latina principals after analyzing the *testimonios* of four Latina school leaders. Their findings revealed the importance of applying a framework that allows for analysis of race and gender. For example, two participants described struggles they faced while trying to navigate motherhood and their careers. Other challenges they faced included hypervisibility and invisibility. The researchers explained:

> When considering that the Latinas were underrepresented in school leadership roles in their respective districts, this often contributed to their hypervisibility, at times resulting in being tokenized, essentialized, or discriminated against, while the underinvestment and undervaluing of some of their skills, contributions, and development simultaneously contributed to their invisibility. (p. 490)

The voices of people whose stories have traditionally not been centered in scholarship informs the scholarship and practice of critical social justice leadership. Evidence of this centering of voices can be seen in the next set of constructs we describe. Acknowledgment of *community cultural wealth* in students and families and communities is typically integrated in paradigms of *social justice leadership* and *advocacy*, which is an element of social justice leadership. *Culturally responsive leadership* is a conceptualization of social justice leadership that centers race and culture, and *Latino Educational Leadership* delineates social justice leadership based on uniquely Latina/o/x perspectives.

COMMUNITY CULTURAL WEALTH

Yosso's (2005) seminal article "Whose culture has capital? A critical race theory discussion of community cultural wealth" is provocative for education scholars and practitioners interested in shifting away from deficit notions of historically marginalized groups toward assets-based understandings of diverse cultures. As evidence of the importance of this article to critical education researchers, as of 2022, the article has been cited over 9,000 times in Google Scholar. Yosso challenged the traditional interpretations of cultural capital theory, developed by Bourdieu. Whereas common interpretations of Bourdieu valued middle and upper middle norms as supporting educational success, Yosso argued that cultural capital is not uniquely possessed by people within middle and upper middle classes. Instead, she asserted the concept of cultural capital typically referred "to an accumulation of specific forms of knowledge, skills and abilities that are valued by privileged groups in society" (p. 76).

Yosso turned to CRT scholarship to guide her conceptualization of a construct that acknowledges forms of capital within marginalized groups. She explained, "CRT identifies various indicators of capital that have rarely been acknowledged as cultural and social assets in Communities of Color" (p. 82). Theorizing about cultural wealth shifts thinking about historically marginalized groups (i.e., people of color or people experiencing poverty) as having deficits, to thinking about attributes that empower those communities.

There are six forms of capital in this framework:

- Aspirational capital—the ability to maintain hopes and dreams for the future;
- Linguistic capital—intellectual and social skills attained through communication in more than one language and/or style that support bi- or multilingualism;
- Familial capital—cultural knowledge developed among kin that informs community history, cultural intuition, broad understandings of kinship as extended family, and a commitment to community well-being;
- Social capital—a reliance on networks of people and community to help navigate and gain access to social institutions;
- Navigational capital—the ability to maneuver through institutions where White, English-speaking, middle-class norms are dominant; and
- Resistant capital—knowledge and skills that challenge inequality and subordination.

Scholars have explored community cultural wealth in a wide range of topics. Examples particular to Latinos include an examination of the ways

Latina/o third-grade students reflect about their use of community cultural wealth through writing *testimonios* (DeNicolo et al., 2015), a Latinx high school teacher's engagement with her students (Martin-Beltrán et al., 2018), how Latino college students used community cultural wealth to navigate college (Duncheon, 2018; Kouyoumdjian et al., 2015; Liou et al., 2009; Luna & Martinez, 2012; Pérez, 2017), and the community cultural wealth of Latina/o parents (Aragon, 2017; Guzmán et al., 2021). Findings typically indicate that Latinos access one or more types of community cultural wealth as they navigate school. These findings are especially important, because they buttress arguments to eschew deficit notions of Latina/o/x students and families.

A common theme in research about Latina/o/x school leaders explores how community cultural wealth inspired Latina/o/x educators to become school leaders. Findings in many studies reveal that Latina/o/x principals who demonstrate social justice leadership practices draw upon their identity to inform their approach for creating and maintaining high academic expectations (e.g., see Hernandez et al., 2014; Murakami et al., 2016). Hernandez et al. (2014) summarized research that highlighted the ways Latina school principals constructed their identities as principals based on their own experiences in schools.

Another theme explores how community cultural wealth informs the leadership practices of Latinx school administrators. Rodela and Rodriguez-Mojica (2020) studied four Latinx school administrators' experiences to understand how their community cultural wealth informs their "equity leadership visions" (p. 290) and their navigation of district equity initiatives. The administrators' experiences as students of color informed their approach to addressing systemic inequities such as racism or deficit ideologies. They contributed to equity by directly serving and advocating for students of color and low-income students of color, despite the tendencies by their districts to promote "generalized equity calls for 'all students to succeed'" (p. 305). The researchers found evidence that all six types of capital informed practices across the four participants. Furthermore, the leaders drew upon their own community cultural wealth in their leadership practice. While the leaders were aware of their "cultural, linguistic, and racial differences to the majority White administrators and teachers in their districts, [they saw] their differences as strengths in serving families in their schools, particularly Spanish-speaking Latinx students and families of color" (p. 310).

Familial Capital

As mentioned earlier, some research focuses on the experiences of women, which sheds light on their experiences at the intersection of their race and gender. Community cultural wealth is a common theme. Familial capital, in particular, is frequently observed in studies about Latina school leaders/administrators. For example, two Latina school leaders studied by Menchaca et al. (2017) were motivated by family support while obtaining their teaching degrees. Additionally, Martinez et al. (2016) analyzed the *testimonios* of four Latina administrators. They concluded, the

> idea of becoming administrators was not an original goal for all participants, but at some point throughout their lives individuals, some family members and/or mentors, and key relationships played a significant role in the development of the participants' leadership goals and styles. (p. 17)

Hernandez et al.'s (2014) examination of the role of racial identity in a Latina principal's leadership beliefs and practices highlighted the importance of familial capital. The principal described how multiple aspects related to her family influenced her. These included her appreciation for her family which "was at the core of her being" (p. 579) and her family's high academic expectations. She also noted how experiences with racism in her own schooling shaped her racial identity and influenced her teaching practices. As a principal, she was committed to dismantling race and class privilege in her school, respecting students and families, developing culturally responsive connections between White teachers and students and families of color, and increasing community and family engagement, particularly for Latino families.

Hernandez and Murakami's (2016b) study of a Latina school principal revealed the ways in which she developed a professional and racial identity. Through counter-storytelling the principal explained the assets from her family and background, such as "Her father was a role-model in developing a financially stable family" (p. 6) and was a role model who valued education.

Finally, six Latina school leaders described their career and mentoring progression (Rodríguez et al., 2018). As with other research, the leaders expressed the importance of their family life, influence of their parents and their background as contributing factors to their leadership trajectories. Consistent with other research as well, the participants expressed how witnessing the racism their parents experienced influenced their leadership.

Navigational Capital

Evidence of Latina/o/x school leaders' navigational capital, which is their ability to maneuver successfully through institutions dominated by White, English-speaking cultural norms, can be seen in their successful matriculation through high school, undergraduate education, and graduate education at the master's level or higher (as most school leadership positions require a master's degree or higher). Additionally, as education professionals, many Latina/o/x school leaders successfully maneuver a professional course from aide, interpreter, or teacher, to school-level or district-level leadership. However, given the underrepresentation of Latinos in leadership positions, we attribute the low numbers in part, to a lack of mentoring opportunities, especially by mentors who share their identity. Increasing scholarship points to the importance of this type of mentorship for prospective Latina/o/x school leaders.

Magdaleno (2006) declared the importance of same-race administrator mentors for improving the probability of success for Latina/o school leaders, as he described a formal mentoring program developed for Latina/o leaders in the California educational system. He identified systemic challenges which contributed to low numbers of Latina/os in school administration. Magdaleno asserted mentoring is one way to overcome those challenges. He pointed out:

> For Latina and Latino educational leaders, mentoring by an experienced educational leader is a priority; mentoring by an experienced educational leader who understands and shares common experiences, a common language, similar racial and equity concerns, and who can also relate to the specific cultural experiences of his or her protégé is even more crucial. (p. 13)

As another example, five Latina/o suburban secondary school principals identified mentors as supports for their career development. Researchers connected this finding to the importance of formal same-race mentorship programs for Latina/o administrators, such as the one developed by Magdaleno in California (Fernandez et al., 2015).

Access to Latina mentors, or lack thereof, was a common theme among research that centers Latina administrators. For example, none of the five school leaders interviewed by Avalas and Sagalo (2016) had a Latina mentor. Latina school leaders studied by Martinez et al. (2020) revealed a lack of mentoring by Latina administrators, due to underrepresentation in the field, as a challenge. Even though the number of Latinas who obtain graduate degrees in education has increased, the number who hold school, district office, or superintendent positions is low (Avalos & Salgado, 2016; Mendez-Morse, 2000, 2004). This results in Latina leaders having to create "cross-race and gender mentoring relationships to help them navigate and advance their careers" (Martinez et al., 2020, p. 490).

Rodríguez et al. (2018) found Latina school leaders identified their mothers as their primary mentors. Other family members were also mentioned as mentors. Professional mentors included Latina/o and White leaders. Some leaders sought mentoring relationships with other administrators, while one leader also sought out and learned from mothers who were part of the school community. Although they mentioned the need to prove their competency due to their gender and race as a barrier to their leadership, the leaders emphasized the importance of building professional networks through organizations and mentoring, as strategies for overcoming those barriers (Rodríguez et al., 2018).

Finally, Murakami et al. (2018) found that Latina/o administrators were aware of their importance as role models for students and adults. The researchers posited that this awareness "was an indication that these administrators were critical in their roles and intentional in their investments to improve the experiences of those in schools" (p. 14).

Linguistic Capital

The ways in which linguistic capital benefits Latinx administrators and their school communities have been explored. An administrator in Martinez et al.'s (2016) study was the first bilingual Spanish and English-speaking Latina administrator on her campus. She "understood her critical role in serving a predominantly Latinx population. . . . Her identity as a Spanish-speaking Latina was vital" for developing relationships and communicating with Latinx parents who may not otherwise talk with non-Spanish-speaking faculty (p. 12). All four leaders in this study expressed how their bilingualism was an asset as a part of their cultural identity, while also sharing how they experienced challenges in mainstream school and society that valued English only. The ways in which Latina principals' cultural understanding of Latino families is an asset, resonates among several other studies. A participant in another study recalled how she was ridiculed because of her accent. However, "by maintaining her home language, she was more accessible to the children and families who shared the same language" (Avalos & Salgado, 2016, p. 28).

Mendez-Morse (2004) also highlighted that all six participants in her study "were proud of their bilingual abilities and had used these, to varying degrees, in their careers" (p. 571). Research in these areas reveals the ways Latina/o/x school leaders draw on their community cultural wealth to enact social justice leadership in their schools.

SOCIAL JUSTICE LEADERSHIP

Principals who are social justice leaders identify and dismantle inequities which result in the marginalization of groups, often due to their race, gender identity, ability, sexuality, immigration status and country of origin, and class (Furman, 2012; Lewis & Kern, 2018; Pounder et al., 2005; Theoharis, 2007). Social justice leadership is "framed as a synthesis of dispositions, values, and practices that are contextually responsive and reflective of the plural nature of social justice" (DeMatthews et al., 2016, p. 759).

Dantley and Tillman (2010) asserted that a social justice leader "investigates and poses solutions for issues that generate and reproduce societal inequities" (p. 19). Therefore, as advocates, social justice leaders engage in actions that create equitable schools (Crawford et al., 2014; DeMatthews et al., 2017; Furman, 2012; Shaked, 2020).

Advocacy

Advocacy includes actions at the individual, institutional (school), and societal levels, *in concert with* historically underserved groups, to promote change within policies, practices, and laws that contribute to the marginalization of certain groups. Emphasis on *in concert with* is important because the voices of people being served must always remain central to decision-making and actions. Social justice advocacy in schools means that such advocacy occurs on behalf of students and families (Marbley et al., 2011). Pounder et al. (2005) explained that social justice leadership requires "understanding that one is not just a leader but an activist for children, an activist who is committed to supporting educational equity and excellence for all children" (p. 272). While school personnel such as teachers or community mentors can exhibit leadership roles essential for student advocacy (Grice & Parker, 2018), we focus on traditional formal school leadership roles.

Scholars have investigated how cultural capital informs the advocacy practices of Latina/o/x administrators (DeMatthews et al., 2016; DeMatthews et al., 2017; Murakami et al., 2016). DeMatthews et al. (2016) explored a Mexican American female school leader's social justice leadership through her advocacy for students and community in Ciudad Juárez, Mexico. They found that the inequities faced by the community "created a social justice leadership imperative focused on authentic family engagement and community solidarity" (p. 756). The school leader's leadership included four key practices that contributed to social justice advocacy:

a) a commitment to "learning about the lived experiences of marginalized communities" and how those experiences impact student well-being;
b) reflective leadership that balances multiple purposes of schooling, including academics, social-emotional well-being for students and families, and community engagement;
c) the rejection of notions that the leader knows all with an investment in parents as "most important to student success"; and

d) the development of socially just school-community partnerships that draw upon families' community cultural wealth.

e) Although this study investigated leadership in an international setting, the ways in which the school leader engaged in community advocacy can be applied in education communities in the United States (p. 784).

In another study of one educational leader, DeMatthews et al. (2017) investigated a Latino superintendent's leadership to implement a dual language model in his district. The superintendent's personal experiences were formative to his belief that dual language programming was important. For example, he was "conscious of the way Mexican and Mexican-American emergent bilinguals were marginalized" (p. 20) from his own experience. In addition to situational awareness, the researchers found that the superintendent engaged in advocacy by implementing district-wide professional development and praxis because he "perceived the various oppressive elements confronting emergent bilinguals and took action" (p. 22).

Conversely, as a result of reviewing educational policies in Utah, Alemán (2009) concluded that "liberal ideology and Whiteness" led Latino/a leaders "to conform to a polite and nonconfrontational rhetoric" (p. 297). He found that the leaders were aware of civil rights shortcomings, yet "fell short of publicly critiquing the standards of Whiteness that these systems reified" (p. 298). Instead, the leaders expressed their belief that being present for policymaking decisions was more effective than "taking 'potshots' at those in power," by directly challenging White privilege and racism. He concluded, the "overbearing *niceness*" . . . [insulated] the participants from considering political discourse shaped by conflict, critique, and a questioning of White privilege" (p. 304, italics original), which ultimately serves to maintain an inequitable status quo.

Murakami et al. (2016) conducted a survey to understand Latina/o principals' identity, and its relationship to their leadership styles and advocacy. This is unique because this quantitative study is one of few in a field where the vast majority of studies are qualitative. Open-ended survey responses to a question about challenges and successes revealed challenges about teacher preparation to prepare students to contribute to society, noting their commitment to democratic practice. Regarding advocacy specifically, one principal identified "the importance of having the opportunity to 'work as an advocate for low socioeconomic students to ensure their success'" (p. 293).

In another study based on survey data, Murakami et al. (2018) asked Latina/o school administrators to consider the intersections between their professional identity, race/ethnicity, and class backgrounds. Their findings revealed that race and class influenced their work as school administrators, which led to the "development of their professional identities" (p. 5).

Leadership on School Boards

Sampson (2019) examined the educational leadership of Latinx school board members to understand whether and how they addressed educational equity. As with P-12 school administrators, the Latinx school board members referenced how their family, identity, and experiences informed their practices to address inequity, and their engagement in a variety of advocacy efforts. Unique to their role as school board members in a political context, they were beholden to communities who either supported or rejected their social justice advocacy efforts. As with superintendents (DeMatthews et al., 2017), Sampson found that coalition-building is important for school board members.

CULTURALLY RESPONSIVE SCHOOL LEADERSHIP

Various pedagogies that center student cultures and experiences share common interests vis à vis social justice. These pedagogies include, but are not limited to: multicultural education (Banks, 1993; Nieto, 2010); culturally relevant (Ladson-Billings, 2009) and culturally responsive (Gay, 2010; Howard, 2010; Villegas & Lucas, 2002) teaching; culturally sustaining (Paris & Alim, 2014) and critical culturally sustaining/revitalizing (McCarty & Lee, 2014) pedagogy. They all seek to increase student engagement, and achievement through reflexive practice, social and political consciousness, and inclusion of diverse students and families.

Aspects of these pedagogies have been applied to educational leadership (Khalifa et al., 2016) in part because, teaching practice alone cannot address structural inequities in schools. Khalifa et al. (2016) explained that culturally responsive leadership "is not only liberatory and antioppressive, it is also affirmative, and seeks to identify and institutionalize practices that affirm Indigenous and authentic cultural practices of students" (p. 1278). The framework consists of four dimensions that are embedded in school leaders' continuous improvement to: (1) critically self-reflect on leadership behaviors; (2) develop culturally responsive teachers; (3) promote a culturally responsive/inclusive school environment, and (4) engage students, parents, and Indigenous contexts. To engage authentically in all of these actions, school leaders must continuously resist deficit notions of students and families and center their voices and experiences (see Khalifa et al., 2016, Table 2, pp. 1283–1284). The Latina/o/x school leaders in this book engaged in culturally responsive school leadership from their unique Latino cultural perspectives.

LATINO EDUCATIONAL LEADERSHIP

The concept of Latino Educational Leadership (LEL) incorporates dimensions from social justice and culturally responsive school leadership frameworks. It centers the unique lived and educational experiences of diverse Latinx communities. Rodríguez et al. (2018) defined LEL as leadership across the P-20 pipeline in the United States that "acknowledge[s] the importance of serving Latino communities and families. Leaders are needed that can meet the needs of the growing and diverse Latino community; leaders who bravely and unapologetically validate and advance cultural, linguistic, and historical connections for Latino communities" (p. 15). This leadership framework acknowledges the unique contributions that Latinx leaders offer and suggests that non-Latino leaders can develop the consciousness and skills to become allies. They elaborated, "The key, which is paramount to the concept of Latino Educational Leadership, is to prepare all leaders to be critical in their practice to serve and empower Latino communities and improve access and equity in schools and educational systems" (p. 15).

> The key, which is paramount to the concept of Latino Educational Leadership, is to prepare all leaders to be critical in their practice to serve and empower Latino communities and improve access and equity in schools and educational systems.
>
> (Rodríguez et al., 2018, p. 15)

Several theories informed the development of LEL. Similar to the evolution of critical race theories described earlier in this chapter, the theories that inform LEL include critical theories derived from Marxist thought, critical race theory, and LatCrit. The authors also were influenced by previously described constructs of deficit thinking, community cultural wealth, and applied critical leadership (Santamaría & Santamaría, 2012; Santamaría, 2014).

Applied critical leadership (ACL) emerged from the authors' research of Indigenous educational leaders in the United States. This construct draws on the positive attributes of a leader's identity that inform their critical approach to leadership, which results in social justice-oriented change. Therefore it "results from both professional practice and leaders' embodied lived experiences" (Santamaría & Santamaría, 2015, p. 26). Rodríguez et al. (2018) made a connection between this framework, which is situated in and derived from research about Indigenous leaders, and Latino Educational Leadership. Santamaría and Santamaría (2012) argued that there are critical leaders who are White and deliberately use a CRT lens to guide their leadership practice. That argument influenced Rodríguez et al. (2018), who asserted that leaders who are not Latinx can advocate for Latinx students and families. They explained:

> We similarly conclude that not only Latinx educational leaders and other school leaders of color, but White educational leaders can purposefully adopt an ACL approach in their practice to effectively meet the needs of Latinx students and families, as well as all others. (p. 8)

We also, argue that White and other school leaders of color can develop critical leadership approaches that center the lived experiences of Latina/o/x students and families as they learn from Latina/o/x students, families, educators, and school leaders.

White and other school leaders of color can develop critical leadership approaches that center the lived experiences of Latina/o/x students and families as they learn from Latina/o/x students, families, educators, and school leaders.

To be sure, it is necessary to hire Latina/o/x school leaders because they bring unique assets, skills, and competencies to increasingly diverse school districts. It is also important for non-Latina/o/x leaders to enact changes that dismantle inequity by centering the experiences of Latina/o/x leaders, what we refer to as "engraving."

Books about Latina/o/x School Leaders

The last thing we do in this chapter is highlight three recent books about Latina/o/x school leaders. Our purpose in doing this is to point the reader toward other books that may be of interest as they continue to explore Latina/o/x school leadership. Two of the books are edited volumes, one of which covers Latino leadership across the P-20 (preschool through college) pipeline. The first, *Brown-eyed leaders of the sun* (Hernandez & Murakami, 2016a) is based on research collected as part of the National Latina/o Leadership Project. Chapters in this book describe, explore, and analyze Latina/o/x school leaders' personal and professional identities and their paths to leadership, cultural assets that contribute to their leadership perspectives, including a commitment to serving parents and families, challenges faced and aspirations, and experiences unique to Latina principals, through a lens of race and gender, which generally support the findings of researchers elsewhere.

Rodríguez et al. (2018) compiled chapters that provide insights into the types of Latino educational leadership that were important in the context of the presidency of Donald Trump. They asserted he ran for the presidency on an anti-immigration agenda that was "not only anti-Mexican, but anti-Latinx at its core" (p. x). Therefore, the Latino leadership beliefs and practices centered in the book explore those qualities among educational leaders across the education landscape from pre-kindergarten through college that will not only "preserve, defend, and fight for social justice in [Latino] communities, but to cultivate the next generation of activists, leaders, scholars, teachers, artists, dreamers, and advocates who will continue to push against destructive ideologies that threaten [Latinos'] very existence" (p. x).

Important findings about the leadership practices of P-12 leaders include the ways in which Latina school leaders in Texas prioritized relationship-building with students, families, and communities, in the pursuit of student achievement (Almager et al., 2018). We contributed a chapter (2018) that described social justice advocacy practices and the factors that informed the leadership of four Latinx education leaders in a midwestern school district. The leaders focused on data, enacted high academic expectations, built staff capacity to discuss race and ethnicity, and created strong relationships with families by prioritizing communication, listening to their experiences, and valuing bilingualism. Factors that influenced their commitment to advocacy for Latinx students and families included their own school experiences, professional experiences prior to leadership, and motivation from their family.

Niño (2018) documented the leadership practices of three male Latino superintendents in Texas. They led with an ethic of care, addressed equity through courageous leadership, and used data. They established *comunidad* (community) through collaborative decision-making; and critiqued their practice through daily reflection. After sharing the findings of the men in his study, Niño contended "more studies need to be done to celebrate the works of women" (p. 71).

Martínez and Méndez-Morse (2021) contributed to that gap with their edited volume. Their book "provides a much-needed space where the voices, stories, experiences, and lives of Latina [P-12] school administrators can be authentically revealed, explored, appreciated, and theorized" (pp. xiv–xv). Chapters include *testimonios* from current and former leaders who explore their experiences through critical race and gender theories to reveal how they drew upon their community cultural wealth to navigate challenges and succeed in their roles. Byrne-Jiménez and Garcia (2021) examined the ways in which Afro-Latina leaders' leadership identities and ability to code-switch are informed by their cultural and familial backgrounds and sisterly bonds. Other chapters highlight community-school leadership (Gil, 2021) and the role of networking and mentoring for Latina school leaders, particularly when there is a lack of formal mentoring programs (Quiñones & FitzGerald, 2021). Finally, Owens and Harris (2021) explored the ways in which community cultural wealth contributed to the career trajectories of Latina school leaders and superintendents. In the next chapter, we explain our research process and introduce the school leaders.

Chapter 2

Introduction to the School Leaders

At the time of our interviews, two leaders, Antonio and Martha, were elementary school principals (grades K-5); one leader, George, was a high school principal (grades 9–12); and four were district-level administrators. Cecilia and Martina were director and executive directors of multilingual and bilingual education departments. Sonia and Velma were associate and elementary superintendents, respectively. Enrique was a former principal who became a consultant and author (see table 2.1).

Antonio grew up in the racially and culturally diverse Logan Square Neighborhood on the north side of Chicago. He described it as a "pretty low-income neighborhood. Very diverse." He grew up around many Hispanics but, "very diverse within the Hispanic group," which included some African Americans and Filipinos. Both of his parents are first-generation immigrants from Mexico. Antonio attended Chicago P-12 public schools, then graduated from the University of Illinois in Chicago. He was a bilingual teacher in Chicago before going into administration. He was an assistant principal for six years in Chicago before taking his first job as head principal of an elementary school in WSD.

Cecilia attended school in Hialeah, a city within greater Miami, Florida. She remembers the push for English language-only in schools beginning in kindergarten, despite speaking Spanish in her home and no school programs to help her learn English. Despite those challenges, Cecilia loved school and always wanted to become a teacher. She taught for ten years in the greater Miami area. Her principal encouraged her to become an elementary reading coach. Eventually she moved to a different city in Florida and took on the role of district-level resource teacher for English language learners, then became the district-level Title III coordinator, then director of the district's Bilingual/ESOL (English for Speakers of Other Languages) office.

Table 2.1   School Leaders' Names, Backgrounds, and Professional Positions

Name (Pseudonym)	Heritage Country of Origin	Place of Birth/Childhood	Positions in P-12 Education	Position Held at Time of Interview
Antonio	Mexico	Chicago, IL; Logan Square Neighborhood	Bilingual teacher; Assistant Principal, Principal	Elementary Principal
Cecilia	Cuba	Hialeah, Greater Miami, FL	Teacher, reading coach, district-level Resource Teacher for ELLs, Title III coordinator, Director of district's Bilingual/ESOL office	Director of district's Bilingual/ESOL office
Enrique	Ecuador	Pico Union area of Los Angeles County, CA	Bilingual teacher's aide, Athletic coach, Elementary school teacher, Community involvement resource teacher, Elementary school principal, Middle School principal, High School principal, Consultant and author	Consultant and author
George	Mexico	Toldeo, OH, and Chula Vista, CA	Special Education teacher, Middle School principal, High School principal	High School principal
Martha	Cuba and U.S.	Milwaukee, WI	Teacher, Bilingual resource teacher, Elementary School principal	Elementary principal
Martina	Argentina	Santiago del Estero, Argentina	Bilingual teacher, Principal, Executive Director of Office of Multilingual and Global Education	Executive Director of Office of Multilingual and Global Education
Sonia	Mexico	Rosarito, Baja California, Mexico	Bilingual teacher, Principal, Associate Superintendent	Associate Superintendent
Velma	Dominican Republic	Jersey City, New Jersey	Bilingual educator, Principal	Elementary Superintendent

Enrique was born and raised in the Pico Union area of Los Angeles County, California. The area is "often referred to as the Ellis Island of the West Coast" due to the large number of Latinx immigrants who come there when they first arrive to the United States. His parents immigrated from Ecuador and his neighborhood growing up was comprised of mostly Mexican Americans. After attending kindergarten at a public school, his parents invested in his education by enrolling him in parochial schools. His first role in education was as a bilingual teacher's aide, then athletic coach, then elementary school teacher, then a community involvement resource teacher for middle- and high school-aged students. As an administrator, Enrique was an assistant principal and principal at all three levels (elementary, middle, and high school), before becoming an education consultant and author.

George and his two siblings grew up living with their father in Toledo, Ohio, during the school year. He described the northwestern Ohio city as a "blue collar, factory, automotive industry" culture. During the summers, the children lived with his mother in Chula Vista, California. George was "only one of a few students of color" in his high school in Ohio, but in the summers when he went to Chula Vista, "it was flipped in which it was predominantly Hispanic, very few Caucasians." After attending college on a baseball scholarship, George became a special education teacher, and eventually principal at a middle school in California, then in Chicago, Illinois. He was a middle school principal in WSD prior to becoming the principal of a high school in WSD.

Martha grew up in a predominantly White, upper-class suburb of Milwaukee, Wisconsin. She described her upbringing as "probably more middle class" in a culture where she passed as White. Her mother is White and from Minnesota and her father is Cuban. After attending one year in a Catholic school, Martha went to a suburban public school district, which was "pretty well-known for producing college-bound students." Martha taught in Portland, Oregon, and New Delhi, India, then came to WSD as a bilingual resource teacher. She pursued a doctorate in education administration at the same time. She was hired as principal of a K-2 elementary school that offers a Spanish dual language immersion program.

Martina grew up in northern Argentina. Her family was connected to the country's "strong native Indigenous population" in a country that consists of Indigenous peoples and many immigrants. Martina attended public school until grade 5 then went to a private school that focused on the humanities and the study of languages. She recalled, "My parents could tell that I was interested in learning languages, so I learned English, French, Latin, and Greek." She attended college to become a teacher of English as a foreign language and business accounting before immigrating to the United States and securing work as a bilingual teacher in WSD. While a teacher, she saw that many of the administrators that she worked with were not bilingual, nor possessed "experiences around immigration," so she wanted to bring her assets to the administrator role. She earned a doctorate and has served as a principal of the district's first K-5 Spanish dual language immersion elementary school, and as the executive director of the office of multilingual and global education.

Sonia was born in Rosarito, Baja California, a city in Mexico which is very close to the southern California border. She recalls the culture shock she endured as an immigrant to Los Angeles as a child. Her small apartment "felt like a jail cell," it did not feel very safe, and they didn't have access to nature. She also had to adjust to a society in which Spanish was not the dominant language. She began her career as a bilingual teacher, then moved into administration as a principal, after realizing the ways administrators had power to access resources, particularly in service to the bilingual students she served. After serving as a principal, she became an associate superintendent.

Velma was born and grew up in northern New Jersey. She attended nine different schools, some public and some parochial, during her K-12 education. Her parents immigrated from Dominican Republic and worked in the textile industry in northern New Jersey. They made sure she lived in safe neighborhoods with access to the best education possible. She taught as a bilingual educator in Compton, California, moved to several other districts, then taught in a large school district in an eastern state, before becoming a principal, then elementary school superintendent.

Next, we explain how we gathered and developed the information to present to our readers. We interviewed eight school leaders in two different phases. During the first phase, we interviewed four leaders within one school district as part of an earlier study (Lowery & Romero-Johnson, 2018). During the second phase, another set of four interviews were conducted with leaders from among Silvia's professional networks.

FIRST PHASE OF INTERVIEWS

We interviewed the only four Latina/o/x school leaders employed at that time within a midwestern district in which we were both previously employed. At the time of the interviews, Kendra had transitioned out of the district after serving as a teacher and administrator, and was an assistant professor outside of the state. Silvia was still employed in the district. Kendra interviewed Silvia as one of the school leaders in the study, since Silvia was still employed there and was the only Latina/o/x central office administrator.

Since four of the eight leaders came from one district, we provide some context about it. As with the names of our school leaders, Williams School

Table 2.2 WSD Student Enrollment by Race/Ethnicity Calculated as Numbers, Percent of Total Student Enrollment and Change, 2005–2006 and 2015–2016

Total Enrollment	School Year 2005–2006 Fall Enrollment		School Year 2015–2016 Fall Enrollment		Change	
	24,452		27,112		+2,660	
Race/Ethnicity	Number	Percent	Number	Percent	Number	Percent
American Indian	149	0.6	93	0.3	−56	−0.3
Asian	2,568	10.5	2,425	8.9	−143	−1.6
Black	5,199	21.3	4,828	17.8	−371	−3.5
Hispanic	2,830	11.6	5,554	20.5	+2,724	+8.9
Pacific Isle*	0	0	16	0.06	+16	+0.06
White	13,706	56.1	11,724	43.2	−1,982	−12.9
Two or More Races*	0	0	2,472	9.1	+2,472	+9.1

*Note: In 2010, the state changed race/ethnicity categories from five to seven, to include the categories of Pacific Isle and two or more races.

District (WSD) is a pseudonym for a district located in a midwestern state. According to the state database, WSD enrollment increased from 24,452 in 2005 to 27,112 in 2015. During that same period, the number of Hispanic (term used in the state database) students enrolled in the district increased by 8.9% (from 11.6% to 20.5%). Latinx students experienced the largest increase of race/ethnic student groups (see table 2.2).

The underrepresentation of Latina/o/x administrators mirrored national trends. During the 2015–2016 school year, four of approximately 110 administrators were Latina/o/x administrators. Three were building administrators (one high school principal and two elementary school principals) and one was a central office administrator. In a district where Latinx students comprised 20.5% of the student population, just 3.6% of district administrators were Latina/o/x.

Evidence that Latinx students in WSD were underserved includes disproportionately low academic test scores and participation in AP exams. For example, during the 2015–2016 school year, the percent of Latinx students who scored proficient or advanced on the state standardized assessment in English language arts was the second lowest (16.4%) among all race/ethnic groups. Data from 2014–2015 indicate that Latinx students had one of the lowest participation rates (8.2%) in Advanced Placement (AP) exams as well as one of the lowest graduation rates (68.4%) (Lowery & Romero-Johnson, 2018).

Kendra interviewed the four leaders. Their pseudonyms are: Antonio, George, Martha, and Martina.

SECOND PHASE OF INTERVIEWS

The second phase of four interviews were conducted after we considered how we could further explore our inquiry into the lived experiences, community cultural wealth, and leadership practices of Latina/o/x administrators. Silvia recalled the culturally affirming experience she had as a cohort member of a national leadership organization for Latino administrators. The organization's mission and vision are to develop a perspective among aspiring school and district leaders that is informed by Latino cultures and experiences so that schools can effectively meet the educational needs of all students, and Latino students in particular. Primary activities of the organization include professional development, networking, and policy advocacy.

Silvia contacted her cohort members and four agreed to participate. Their pseudonyms are Cecilia, Enrique, Sonia, and Velma. Interviews were conducted via phone and Zoom because we all lived in different states and because these were conducted during the height of the COVID-19 pandemic. Silvia interviewed Cecilia, Sonia, and Velma. Kendra interviewed Enrique.

We met several times to analyze the interviews and identify themes that emerged. Our discussions included our interpretations and reflections about content, the writing process, language, and application to existing research about Latina/o/x school leaders.

Now that you've been introduced to the leaders, the next chapters present counternarratives, or *testimonios,* of their personal and professional lived experiences. Our hope is that you can make connections between their experiences and the concepts we outlined in chapter 1.

Chapter 3

Community Cultural Wealth

Lessons from Childhood, Family, and Community

The school leaders describe how different types of community cultural wealth influenced their leadership practices. The chapter is divided into sections that are labeled with a form of capital as identified by Yosso (2005). Each section begins with a narrative by a leader which exemplifies the form of capital. That is followed by a reference to Yosso's definition of the capital and other narratives to further explore the form of capital. We hope that this format further enriches your understanding of the concepts of community cultural wealth, while engaging you, the reader, with the rich narratives of our school leaders.

You may notice that various forms of capital overlap. For example, aspirational and familial capital often overlap in the narratives. Yosso acknowledged that these forms of capital are not "mutually exclusive or static" (p. 77); they build upon each other. The chapter includes questions for you to deepen your understanding about the content and to consider how you might engrave (apply or implement/incorporate into your practice) lessons from the lived experiences of the school leaders. That is, we want you to consider how you might show evidence that these narratives are not presented solely for informational purposes. Rather, we hope that through reflection and application, these stories become a source of influence on your beliefs and practices to equitably serve Latina/o/x students and families.

ASPIRATIONAL CAPITAL

Enrique: My mother raised us [and] made it so that we never gave up. She made us believe that we were capable of anything. In her parenting, she wanted my brother and I to know that we were capable of anything as long as we tried, and

41

as long as we got up. I often say that my mom might not have a college degree, but she has a PhD in domestic engineering, because she did really, really well when it came to raising us, keeping us safe, avoiding, you know, those vices that end up ruining lives. She was very, very good at that. My father is my best friend and he was incredible at just going after goals. So, my dad is the first to graduate from college. Because he came here as an immigrant but he ended up graduating from Cal State Los Angeles, as a civil engineer. And I was at his graduation, I must have been eight years old when he graduated. But it was really cool, because I think that end[ed] up planting a seed subconsciously in my mind about graduating one day, and [becoming the] first in the family to go after a PhD. And I think that they had a lot to do with that both directly and indirectly.

Aspirational capital refers to the ability to maintain hopes and dreams for the future, even in the face of real and perceived barriers. This resiliency is evidenced in those who allow themselves and their children to dream of possibilities beyond their present circumstances, often without the objective means to attain those goals. (Yosso, 2005, p. 78)

Enrique's reflection about his parents' commitment to his dreams are examples of his family's aspirational capital. He described his parents' beliefs about their children's possibilities and the steps taken to support their education. This type of wealth was articulated by other leaders, as they reflected upon the high expectations that were ingrained in them and the ways their parents taught them they could be anything they wanted to be. Leaders reflected upon their rich familial bonds, specifically their parents, who loved them, supported their aspirations, and supported their access to high-quality education to achieve their goals.

High Expectations

Cecilia: My parents instilled in us that education was the key to, you know, have a place in society, to stand our ground, to support ourselves, to start our families. So yes, they pushed us.

For Cecilia's parents, it wasn't good enough to have an education—her parents also expected their children to do their best in school. Martina's parents also made education a priority through their examples and by investing in her education.

Martina: I grew up in Northern Argentina, in a city called Santiago del Estero. And my mom was a teacher, my dad was a journalist, and we grew up in a working-class home, but with a great emphasis on schools, and learning, and reading. And I initially went to a public school until grade five, it was a very good public school that was part of what we call teacher preparation schools. They're at the tertiary level, they're not universities, but they're certainly post-secondary in that those are the teacher preparation schools. And those schools have an elementary and secondary school where all of the student teachers practice becoming teachers, so that was the public school that I attended.

As Velma and Enrique thought about their parents' roles in their education, they spoke about the "sacrifice" their parents made to ensure access for their children. Velma's *testimonio* reveals the multiple factors her family navigated around schools: working jobs, communicating in an English-dominant school system, and living in a physically safe community.

Velma: My mom more than my dad, my dad was much more traditional, you know, working two, three double shifts. And then my mom who also worked, would be working but also a little bit more [involved in] the schooling part. And her English was—she felt more confident in her English. So, she would be the front-facing person for the schools. And we're very lucky that my mom was never shy. *Como mucha persona* (She had a personality). She may have had an accent, but she was like, "*A mi entienden*" (You will understand me)— they will understand her. So she would always go to the school. And whenever she noticed the school was not at par to her expectations, especially around, I don't know if she would have called it rigor, but learning maybe? And safety. Those were two things that she always looked for. And whenever she worried about one, the other, or both, she would have us move to different schools. And a couple of places where we lived, the public schools just didn't have those two things that she was looking for. So then she would have us go to the local Catholic school, which tended to be back then- I don't know about now- but [tuition was charged on a scale] depending on your income, for the most part. Because I remember her speaking to the head nun—back then there were nuns that were the principals of the school—and really, you know, saying "I have five children. And I really"—and giving that passionate explanation of why she felt they needed to be there. And I will say that it was a sacrifice. They still paid. But you know, they made those sacrifices [for] our education.

Velma explained how her mom and dad invested in her education economically by paying tuition at Catholic schools, by paying attention to the quality of neighborhoods and school systems, and by her mom's fortitude interacting with school officials with the expectation that she would be understood. Rather than viewing her accent as a deficit, Velma's mom knew that school officials who could only speak English needed to build their capacity to understand her.

Velma also reflected on the intersection between her parent's dedication to providing education and safety for her:

> Two things. One, this united, almost singular idea of, we have to find the best school that we can, within their understanding of this crazy [school] system. And then number two, we have to make sure that we continue to fight for their safety, too. So their safety and their education—it was always those two things.

Ultimately, she realized "the emphasis and importance that they placed on [her] own education, and how that absolutely changed the trajectory of [her] life."

Enrique's parents also invested in his attendance at Catholic (parochial) schools. He recognized the importance of their sacrifice for him.

> Now my parents are immigrants from Ecuador, South America and they invested heavily in me going to parochial school. So I actually went to a Catholic elementary school. At the time, I remember my parents making out the tuition, it was $65 a month, which back then was not cheap. Kindergarten was public school. And then after that, my parents decided that we're going to sacrifice and put both of our sons through Catholic elementary, middle, and high school. And so that's where I got started.
>
> I experienced success academically because I understood that especially early on I had been granted two great parents that were willing to help me with my schoolwork and emphasize the importance of studying and doing well in school. I had that privilege of having been born into that kind of family.

Plainly stated, Enrique recognized the relationship between his success in school and his parents' investment in him.

George stressed another aspect of aspirational capital while reflecting about his childhood:

> When [my parents] divorced, they divorced at a relatively young age. My mom, she was still an active part. Dad, as a truck driver, he made decent money and he wasn't home, but when he was, we had things. My mom had about twenty different jobs. She was a secretary working at a library, she worked in a gas station. The main reason we stayed with my dad is because my mom couldn't afford having us there, but we'd go back during the summers and we would stay with my aunts and uncles and stay with my mom. There's times that mom didn't have a place to stay. That was something which we identified [as we got older]. My mom worked like nobody's business, harder than anybody that I know, and I think that that's where all three of my siblings and myself got our work ethic.

George, whose parents were divorced, grew up living in two cities. He lived with his dad in Ohio during the academic year and with his mom in

California during the summers. His observations about his mother reveal the example she set for him regarding a work ethic and survival in the United States. As seen in the *testimonios* of the leaders, aspirational capital was operationalized through the examples parents set for their children.

CONTENT QUESTION

• Review Yosso's definition of aspirational capital. What key words in the school leaders' *testimonios* best resonate with the definition of aspirational capital?

FAMILIAL CAPITAL

Velma: And even though we lived in these communities that were ravaged by so many things, especially because of poverty and crime, and crime because of poverty. I want to be clear, it's poverty. We were very insulated by our parents. And I bring that to my work. I bring the assumption that it's not easy. The assumption that for our communities, our communities that are immigrant communities, first generation communities, communities that have to struggle [with] the system, that it's not easy. So, when they enter a school, or they enter a space where I have any kind of leadership role whether as a teacher when I was a teacher, as an administrator, when I became an administrator, as a principal, as a school superintendent, my number one duty is to do right by families. And to do right by them is to understand what their goals are for their children, and to help them reach those goals, whatever those are. Not to make assumptions about anything. And that was a lesson learned from home.

> *Familial capital* refers to those cultural knowledges nurtured among *familia* (kin) that carry a sense of community history, memory and cultural intuition. This form of cultural wealth engages a commitment to community well being and expands the concept of family to include a more broad understanding of kinship . . . familial capital is nurtured by our "extended family," which may include immediate family (living or long passed on) as well as aunts, uncles, grandparents, and friends who we might consider part of our *familia*. (Yosso, 2005, p. 79, italics original)

Although Velma experienced challenges in her communities as a child, she was nonetheless committed to community well-being as a leader. She connected her lived experience with her current leadership practice. Specifically, she articulated how her experience informs her asset-based perspective about the efforts of immigrant and Latino families to participate in school. Velma's shared experiences with many of the families she serves, informs her tireless approach to doing all she can to help them achieve their educational goals. In this way, her dedication to serving all families in communities with whom she identifies so closely, indicates that the students and families are her *familia*.

Antonio explained how his experiences in a diverse neighborhood in Chicago developed his appreciation for diverse communities and anchored his commitment to community well-being:

> I grew up in the northwest side of Chicago, in a neighborhood called Logan Square. So Logan Square back then was a pretty low-income neighborhood. Very diverse. It's mostly [the] Hispanic group, but very diverse within the Hispanic group. I grew up around Mexicans, Puerto Ricans, some Cubans. There [were] some African Americans and a pretty large amount of Filipinos at that time. Now it's gentrified, so it's a little bit different. And I think for the most part, I attended Chicago public schools throughout all of my elementary and high school. So most of my upbringing was around a low-income, pretty diverse population. The elementary school I went to was pretty diverse, so I was surrounded by multiple cultures within the Hispanic culture. I grew up around Puerto Rican, Mexican, Cuban, African American, White, and then I also mentioned [a] Filipino population. One of the things too that, growing up in elementary school [was] that we were really brought up to really give back to the community. So I think that's something that really shaped my values and my direction and going into education, is really having that sense of when you become someone, or you are in a career, that you always come back to the community and give back. That's part of my larger philosophy, too.

Like Velma and Antonio, Enrique talked about the strength of his community and how it shaped his cultural identity development. While others may have focused on the crime that existed, he emphasized the richness of the cultural diversity:

> I grew up in the Pico Union area of Los Angeles County. Born and raised there, often referred to as the Ellis Island of the West Coast, because so many Latinx immigrants come to that part of Los Angeles when they're just starting out. It is a community that had its challenges, obviously, a lot of economic challenges. And that led to other challenges with regard to crime and gangs and that sort of thing. But I loved it. I'll be honest with you, I still go back once in a while. I enjoy traveling through there. I enjoy having lunch there. I enjoy taking people there. It's very rich and diverse. When I was growing up it was mostly a Mexican American community or a Mexican community. Now it's more El Salvadoran.

He recounted what he appreciated about his community:

> I really appreciated growing up in a very rich and mostly Latinx [community], but there was a lot of other diversity. I mean, my neighbors from across the street were half Japanese, half Peruvian, many of my friends were Mexican American, my family's friends were mostly South American. There [were] many Central Americans. In fact, my wife is from El Salvador. And so I ended up marrying someone from Central America. I loved the fact that we were, it was a rough neighborhood, but we were all family. You know, if somebody got in trouble, other people would be there for you. And I never grew up with this idea of being a minority. We were the majority. I mean, to me, majority meant there's more of us than [other races]. And [I] just loved the sense of family and culture and language that we were all part of. And that's something that I'm very grateful for 'til this day. I didn't grow up wondering what it's like to be Latino. I grew up embracing that part of our culture. And I love it—I love that experience.

In his *testimonio*, Enrique identified elements of the familial capital he developed while growing up in his neighborhood. He invoked the words "family" and "love," indicating that this part of his upbringing played a role in shaping his identity and thus, his leadership.

CONTENT QUESTION

• Review Yosso's definition of aspirational capital. What key words or passages in the school leaders' *testimonios* best resonate with the definition of aspirational capital?

Familial Capital and Immigration Experiences

Every school leader honored the rich legacy of their and/or their family's immigration experiences. Those experiences enhanced their ability to understand and advocate for Latina/o/x students and families because they understood Latina/o/x immigrant experiences from personal or familial perspectives.

Sonia was born in Rosarito, Baja California, in Mexico, which is about an hour and half journey between California and Mexico. She remembers there was one school with four classrooms, one hotel, and a dairy farm. She has fond memories of running around the farm, noting, "Sometimes I would help get the cows in line to get milked." Her family moved to the United States because, "if you had a family member who had been born in the U.S., they could sponsor the rest of the family." So they moved to a small apartment in Los Angeles. The transition required adjusting to new environmental and material circumstances. By comparison, the new apartment was "a shock [and] felt like a jail cell." Sonia said the city they migrated to did not have access to nature and she remembers that it "wasn't super safe."

Cecilia was born in the United States but her parents immigrated from Cuba when she was quite young. Reflecting on the cultural differences between the United States and Cuba, she noted, "Even though I was born and raised here, I still came from a home where, you know, we were first generation Americans. So, my household was still very traditional Hispanic, Cuban." Enrique's parents immigrated from Mexico and he recalled memories of growing up in a neighborhood comprised of mostly Latinx immigrants.

Antonio's parents are also first-generation immigrants from Mexico. He "felt very good and strong about [his] culture" and, like Enrique, appreciated growing up within the amalgamation of diverse immigrant communities in his neighborhood. He explained:

> I always say that I'm not your typical Mexican, because I think sometimes my culture is rooted in the Hispanic culture. I know a lot about the Puerto Rican culture, Cuban culture, Dominican Culture, because those were cultures that were around me. My Mom is very Mexican, first-generation. She cooks Cuban food, she makes Puerto Rican food. So it's something that was immersed even within our family. But yeah, it has really helped to shape my understanding too of different cultures around me, and really helped me to understand the importance of really understanding the other cultures to really give everybody a fair chance as far as who we are.

George's mother is from Juárez, Mexico. Her family "went back and forth [between the U.S. and Mexico] pretty freely, but she was documented." His dad, who is from Chihuahua, Mexico, was an undocumented immigrant. George recalled:

> My dad was a truck driver, he did automotive work, but he was undocumented. And back in the day that was always something we had to worry about, when they would come in and do their sweeps because in Northwest Ohio there's a lot of farm land and a lot of migrant workers. We always had to be concerned about dad being picked up. My brother, my sister, and I were all born in the United States, and so we were citizens. That was always on our mind.

George spoke about the impact having a father who was undocumented had on his childhood. Because of his experiences, he related to the anxiety that undocumented families might feel, as well as the emotional toll that worrying about a caregiver being deported may have on some of his students. He also recalled the pity among his teachers which led to deficit views about his family, because people knew his father's undocumented status:

My dad spoke very little English. He would, on occasion—I can count on one hand, the times that he walked into my high school or into my elementary school—because of his language barrier he just wasn't comfortable with coming into schools. Teachers often felt bad for my brother, my sister, and myself. Ironically, now my brother has gone on to be pretty successful, my sister, she's the youngest associate dean in Ivy League history, and I think I'm doing pretty well myself. But we struggled when we were younger. I struggled when I was younger. I was able to get into honors and AP classes, but I was basically gifted it because I was a pretty nice kid.

Martina's perspective about her immigrant experience was different from the others because of the sociocultural context of immigration in Argentina, where she was born, and because she was the only participant who immigrated to the United States as an adult. First, she explained, "Argentina has had, historically, a lot of immigration. At the time that I was growing up, it was more second, third-generation families of immigrants. My family doesn't necessarily have a connection with immigrants to Argentina." Further, although she heard occasional stories of her ancestors having roots in Spain, they were never concrete. The family members she has met "were all from Argentina with native indigenous roots."

Martina reflected:

After I immigrated into the U.S., I realized that I am positioned now in a different place. A different type of identity emerged. One as an immigrant, which I didn't have obviously when I lived in Argentina as part of the population of Argentina, kind of a minority-majority population within Argentina. Now I became an immigrant into the U.S., understanding the role of language of Spanish as not the majority language anymore, and that there were different perceptions about the Spanish language. In some places or in some locations, [it had] a lesser hierarchy than English, and yet I still needed it [for] communicating with my family, and then in encountering the enrollment of Spanish speakers within public school.

Martina immigrated to the United States after college. As an adult, she had the wisdom and hindsight to reflect on the importance of the Spanish language in relation to power.

Velma thought about her family's "immigrant story" as a direct connection to her work as a school leader. Her parents immigrated from Dominican Republic and worked in the textile industry. She remembers traveling back and forth to Dominican Republic every summer. As a leader who witnessed many cultural celebrations in schools, Velma wondered, "What does it mean to celebrate beyond like, just celebration? How do we move from that into culturally responsive practice?" She recounted how she created interest among her colleagues:

I shared a little bit of my family's immigrant story . . . I connected it to our families in [my city], the work that we do, and that if you want to celebrate Latinx people or Latino people or Latino heritage, just look around you. Look to your right, look to your left, you know, look at the people that you work with, within the organization and the communities that you serve. And that these stories are . . . My story is the story of the children of [city] and the families of [city] and our colleagues.

Velma's *testimonio* reveals how she was able to model possibilities for inclusion because she related to the immigration experiences of her families.

Martha describes herself as biracial, whose "father is Cuban [and] mother is American [White], from Minnesota." Martha said that she passes as White. She explained, "I would say that I very easily pass as White, so if you did not know me or my family you wouldn't know that I was Latina." Martha's father immigrated from Cuba and received asylum upon his arrival with his parents (Martha's grandparents) when he was a boy. He lived an upper middle-class lifestyle. She explained:

Both of my grandparents went to University of Havana. They were pretty well educated. They came to the States. They were sponsored by the Catholic Church. They moved up to Illinois, and they both worked for John Deere. And my dad was raised middle-upper class. And there was never any real hardship financially. Emotionally, I don't even know the extent of that with my grandmother, but my dad's always found a lot of pride in being Cuban. He's been back to Cuba several times. But my grandmother has always had this air of "We're not the same as them" [other Latinos].

Many of the administrators draw upon their immigration experiences as a source of shared experience with Latino students and families. Martha was adept at analyzing her own privilege as she reflected upon the experiences of her students and families. She recognized that although she is a child of immigrants, her family context was atypical of the experiences of most of the families she served: "My dad was given asylum the second day he stepped onshore in Miami. So, we never had to worry about any sort of immigration, or anything like that."

This was not said with pity. Rather, Martha's reflection underscores why it is essential for school leaders to seek to understand families, rather than compare them in judgment. She continued, "I had a lot of privilege just growing up in [the city I grew up in], having the experience to be exposed and to go to school in that school district. And my parents supported me through undergrad." Martha thought that her parents being divorced made her more different from her peers than her being Latina since she could pass for White.

Relatedly, she understood the implications of being able to "choose" being a Latina:

So I think I kind of straddled that. My mom says it was a convenience thing. I can choose to be Latina when I wanna be Latina, and I very much can also just pass as being White, so super privileged. In that capacity, I get the privileges that come with affirmative action, and with diversifying a workforce [but I am] culturally very different than my Mexican students, primarily. And even the Puerto Rican students, I'd say the majority of my students are Mexican, but there's a couple of Puerto Rican kids, but the experience is so different.

The administrators' Latinx heritages and experiences provided them with a unique perspective borne from experience, which was an asset as they supported students and families.

CONTENT QUESTION

• What similarities and differences exist between the leaders' immigration experiences? In what ways are those similarities and differences manifested in their leadership?

Linguistic Capital

Martina: After fifth grade I moved into a private school, that was sixth through twelfth grade with a focus on the humanities; so we studied a lot of languages, which was exactly what my passion was. My parents could tell that I was interested in learning languages, so I learned English, French, Latin, and Greek in that school for seven years, and lots of literature, lots of philosophy, and the regular high school courses with math, science, etcetera. So it was a very, very good experience for me. Because I have a background in both world languages and I was bilingual, and also I have had a lot of classes in math because I have gone into accounting and business, the shortest route for me to become a teacher was to become a bilingual math teacher, which is what I did. So I became a bilingual math teacher first, and I started working in the WSD at the time of rapid enrollment, both in enrollment of bilingual children and the growth with the language program. I [became] a principal in a language school. Skills that I have that may have been valuable or not, depending on the context, became really, really valuable [My language skills were] really great assets at a time when it was very important to have bilingual teachers and bilingual administrators, and I was so much an asset. So those skills that I had developed were assets that were needed.

> Linguistic capital includes the intellectual and social skills attained through communication experiences in more than one language and/or style. . . Linguistic capital reflects the idea that Students of Color arrive at school with multiple language and communication skills. (Yosso, 2005, p. 78)

Martina demonstrated an aptitude for multiple languages and was supported by her parents to develop them. The school districts in which she worked quickly identified her skills as assets, and she has used her skills to serve families and students. While Martina developed proficiency in multiple languages, most of the school leaders interviewed, demonstrated linguistic capital as bilingual speakers of Spanish and English. They developed their bilingualism despite being pressured to speak English at school.

Velma noted that her identity was rooted in her family and their value of the Spanish language because, "even though at school I was told I could only speak English, at home, my parents were very clear '*aqui no sabe Ingles.*' (You cannot speak English.) So, I definitely lived that duality." She continued:

Even though when you're young, it feels very heavy, I feel like as you grow in yourself, and in your self-identity . . . my cultural and ethnic identity feels very solid. And that's also a process [of] self-awareness. I feel so lucky that I have the richness of my language and my culture at my fingertips. And that every summer, going back and forth to Dominican Republic, really solidified that. *Pasando tiempo con mi abuelita* (spending time with my grandmother) and how I bring all of that to my students.

Reflecting upon her journey as a bilingual student, Velma did not dismiss the struggles she encountered as an emerging English speaker on the way to a robust sense of identity and culture that she genuinely appreciates and shares with her students.

Even though Enrique described most of his teachers as assimilationist who did not celebrate his cultural heritage, he recalled one third-grade teacher who understood his linguistic capital due to him being bilingual in Spanish and English. He remembered,

She was a White woman from Wisconsin, later on became a nun. [She] told me that I needed to embrace my Spanish, because one day, I would be twice as smart as everyone else because I knew two languages. I mean, that was pretty powerful.

As stated previously, Latina/o/x administrators are not a monolithic group. Their backgrounds and experiences are varied. Consider Martha's *testimonio* about language:

I think that the understanding of what it means to be bicultural was not—It wasn't discouraged by my family by any means, but it was just a way of life for us. So, my dad spoke Spanish with my grandparents. I did not speak Spanish until I went . . . as an AFS [originally the American Field Service exchange program] student. When I was 16, I went down to Chile for a while. So my dad never spoke to us in Spanish. He didn't think that culturally it was appropriate.

Although she came to value bilingualism, Martha did not grow up in a home where speaking Spanish was encouraged—at least by her father. As language and culture are tightly coupled, Martha's cultural identity was shaped by this reality. She explained that for her dad, after living in Cuba, speaking Spanish in Wisconsin did not make sense to him, and so they did not speak Spanish. She also noted, "My grandmother would say that it was because of my mom, but my mom never held us back from speaking Spanish." Nonetheless, her sister understands Spanish and won't speak it. Martha describes her own bilingualism as, "I speak it pretty fluently, but it was self-motivated and self-learned, so I learned it through my schooling."

Linguistic capital is evident in the leaders' *testimonios*, however, their development of bi- and multilingualism was not the same. The ways in which Latina/o/x administrators manifested the aspirational, familial, and linguistic capital that emerged from their lived experiences underscores the importance of their familial and cultural heritage. This does not mean that there were not challenges; rather, it means that the challenges did not outweigh their access to quality education that served as a foundation for their careers and service. Further, those challenges did not dominate how they frame their childhoods, heritage, and lived experiences.

CONTENT QUESTIONS

- What aspects of the leaders' development of linguistic capital confirmed or challenged your existing knowledge? Explain.
- As you read the *testimonios*, did you make connections to multiple forms of cultural capital? If so, which ones?
- Did you make connections to forms of capital we did not identify? If so, which ones?

As Yosso (2005) asserted, the purpose of identifying community cultural wealth is not to find "new ways to co-opt or exploit the strengths of Communities of Color. Instead, community cultural wealth involves a commitment to conduct research, teach and develop schools that serve a larger purpose of struggling toward social and racial justice" (p. 82). In response to this call, we offer some reflection questions so that you can apply what you've read and thought about to your practice.

REFLECTION QUESTIONS FOR LEARNING FROM THE EXPERIENCES OF LATINA/O/X SCHOOL LEADERS: ENGRAVING

Latina/o/x school leaders spoke with great admiration about their parents and neighborhoods. These cultural influences, which were vital to their upbringing, informed their leadership.

1. What is one question you can ask students and families that you serve that will inform your understanding of various forms of community cultural wealth?
2. In what ways does understanding the value Latina/o/x leaders place upon their community, heritage, and family serve as a starting point for you to unpack uninformed assumptions you have made about Latina/o/x families and/or immigration experiences?
3. How have these assumptions informed your practice? What is an important next step for you to address these assumptions and resulting practices?
   a. How does learning about the diversity of backgrounds and experiences of the Latina/o/x administrators inform your thinking about Latina/o/x peoples?
   b. How have any deficit notions you hold about Latina/o/x peoples been challenged by reading the *testimonios*?

Questions to Consider About the Hiring Process

4. How might you ascertain the community cultural wealth of Latina/o/x applicants during the hiring process?
5. How might you communicate to Latina/o/x applicants that your school community values the community cultural wealth Latina/o/x leaders may bring?
6. How do you, or can you assess the extent to which applicants value the community cultural wealth of the families they serve or will serve in your school and district?

Chapter 4

The Pathway to Leadership
Motivations and Steps Taken

In the first part of this chapter, leaders describe what motivated them to pursue formal leadership degrees and positions. In the second part, we explain the professional steps they took to achieve their professional goals.

MOTIVATIONS

"A Tap On the Shoulder"
When reflecting on how she became interested in leadership, Martina recounted:

> What's interesting is that—I don't know if it's just my personality—but whatever situation I'm in, I'm called to step up, and it's my nature to want to help. So whether I was a teacher, I would immediately be asked to be a department chair. And if I was a teacher-leader, I would be asked, "Have you ever considered becoming an administrator?" And when I was an administrator, "Have you considered taking the principalship?"

Cecilia's narrative about her pathway to leadership also includes her principal "tapping" her to become a reading coach:

> I always wanted to be a teacher. I was a classroom teacher for ten years. The principal at the school that I taught, I guess he saw something in me, and he tapped me to be the reading coach at the elementary level. And about a year into that position, the district opened district level resource teacher positions in the English Language Learner department. And so I applied. I thought, "Well, you

know, I'll apply," and I got the job. And that led me into being at the district. Even though I was a resource teacher, I really started to like having the ability to interact with teachers [and] principals.

Cecilia's supervisor communicated his belief in her potential, which led to self-recognition of her leadership strengths. Eventually, Cecilia's director was told by her counterpart in another city about an open position. The colleague said:

"I have a position for a title three coordinator. Do you have anybody on your staff that might be interested?" And my director at the time . . . Again, people see in you what you don't see in yourself, right? So, she said to me, "I don't wanna lose you, but this is a great opportunity for you to go to a new district and really expand your leadership role." So I did. I got the job.

The phrase "a tap on the shoulder" in the context of educational leadership refers to a personal invitation to consider becoming a leader by a mentor or someone in a leadership role (McNair, 2014; Tooms, 2007). Tooms (2007) explained that the recipient of such an invitation may not be considering such a move, until asked directly, "Have you ever thought about becoming a school administrator? You would be a good one" (p. 8). Interestingly, Martina recalled the "taps" she received from district leaders that used the same language in the questions posed by Tooms. That interaction could be the catalyst which builds their interest, confidence, and ignites their pursuit of leadership. The extent to which these "taps" influence professionals, such as teachers, to seek leadership positions in general, as well as the types of "taps" and extent to which they influence Latinx leaders are under-researched (Rodela et al., 2019; Tooms, 2007). Evidence from Martina and Cecilia suggests these "taps" played a role in their pursuit of leadership. At the same time, it is important to note that the leaders demonstrated their potential to be excellent leaders while in their current role, which led to being tapped on the shoulder.

HIGH EXPECTATIONS

A desire to instill high expectations and increase educational opportunities motivated some of the school leaders to pursue administration. Conversely, a desire to eradicate the low expectations and deficit-thinking they were recipients of as students, was also a source of motivation.

Uplifting High Expectations

Although Enrique originally entered education simply because he wanted to earn enough money to buy cars, he realized his calling was to facilitate equitable learning opportunities for students. He explained that once he started working,

> I fell in love with kids. I've always had an admiration for kids of all shades, kids of all backgrounds, and just how much innocence and promise they bring to the world. And how society ends up screwing them up somehow, you know, with thoughts that are not necessarily inclusive of that innocence, and that truthfulness, that transparency. And so when I worked with these kids after getting the job, I saw that this was not just about learning, it was about making it. Are we going to be able to give them what they need so that they are able to make it? And that definition of "making it" has changed over the years but today it means having limitless possibilities to do whatever they want to do and be happy doing it. Having the knowledge and skills to be able to do that. So, to me, this has always been personal. I seek out schools that have the, I often refer to as the kids that society says aren't going to make it. I want to work with the low income kids, I want to work with the Black kids, the brown kids, I want to work with the immigrant kids.

Eradicating Low Expectations

Antonio and George recalled schooling experiences that they bring to their leadership roles in order to ensure they do not happen for their students. They remembered that teachers felt sorry for them, which led to low expectations and them not being prepared for college. Antonio recalled that upon going to college, he realized that he lacked requisite skills: "I didn't feel that I was prepared with the writing and critical thinking skills that I needed to be successful." Once he became a teacher, he decided to become an administrator because he wanted to raise expectations and standards for bilingual classrooms in the predominately Latino schools in which he worked. He recounted, "I was a bilingual teacher and really realized that I needed to impact education in a different way, just because the bilingual and the educational systems for that population [were] not as strong."

Desire to Contribute Linguistic Capital As a Bilingual Educator

Martina realized that she was more competent in meeting the needs of bilingual and Latinx students than the current district administrators because of her leadership skills and linguistic capital as a bilingual educator. Therefore, she wanted to impact district-wide practices. She reflected:

> It's interesting because part of it was me having an interest, but part of it was the situation that I was in, where there was truly a lack of leadership. And so, most of the administrators that I worked with as a bilingual teacher were not bilingual themselves, were not also from a Latino/Hispanic background, did not have experiences around immigration, and many of them were supportive in general, but just had not come from that background.

Martha had similar thoughts about her level of competency. She recalled:

> I think that I always thought that I could probably do it better than the administrators that I had, and that was probably the push. I left [a job] because I didn't feel like I was professionally being challenged enough. But I've always been interested in leadership. I did that in high school for quite a while. I was on the student council, and enjoyed that work, and enjoy pushing people to change. And I think at some point I just realized that nobody that was administrating me had any knowledge that I didn't have, and that I should go for it.

Power to Enact and Influence Advocacy

A desire to advocate for equitable school practices and policies motivated some of the leaders to enter school leadership. They believed formal leadership positions yielded more institutional power. Sonia's explanation of her route to leadership exemplifies this. She started her education career as a fourth and fifth grade teacher in a bilingual classroom. Upon reviewing the teaching materials, she was dissatisfied because they did not authentically represent the way her students talked. She approached the principal and said, "I don't speak this way and the kids don't speak this way." The principal said, "Fine don't use them. Tell me what you need." Sonia remembered, "that taught me that administrators have a lot of power."

As she thought about her leadership journey, Sonia elaborated on the complexities of navigating cultural identity, racism, advocacy, and her desire to enact decisions she felt were critical for student success. She said, "I think I suppressed my cultural identity for many years, but I could not suppress my voice. I was fired from my job because I spoke publicly." That incident occurred when she was a literacy coach and challenged the implementation of standardized curriculum. She determined that she "needed to be more careful, but that drove me to become an AP [assistant principal]". Similarly, in response to why she became an administrator, Velma stated, "I wanted to impact more. And I wanted to influence policy."

Increased Representation of Latinos in Leadership

Velma and George articulated a desire to increase the number of Latinos in leadership as a motivating factor for their pursuit of leadership roles. Velma said she was motivated because "there are not enough of us." She explained that she plans to interview Latina leaders in education for her doctoral research. When she identified a potential district for her study, she was surprised to learn

> there are none. There's no—there's not one Latina principal. They don't have any. It's not a tiny district. It's a medium sized district And when we interviewed the superintendent to ask him about it, he stopped and he looked at me, and he said, "I have a lot of work to do." So I expanded my view of leadership, which I think is appropriate. Teacher leaders, coaches, you know, I expanded it. Yeah, so that was a rude awakening. There's a lot that needs to improve in [my current district]. But I will say, having been in [my current district] the longest, I do take for granted that I can find myself [Latina leaders], you know? So, I think one, because there weren't enough of us inspired me. I was like, Why aren't there—? I don't see any Latinas.

Speaking about his experiences, George reflected:

> I sit and I look at the way that we do things here in WSD, and we don't have many models for any of our students of color. We have very few. And that, in essence, really in my opinion hurts. It hurts some of our students of color in which they don't have that role model or mentor or whatever you might call it. They don't have that in the schools. And when they do, and I'm saying this as being somebody who was fortunate enough to go to college through sports, it's usually only linked through sports. Whether as a coach, which is great. But still, I need kids to see that you can do all these other things and you can do it 'cause I could do it. And we can sit down and try to support you to get there.

To summarize, factors that motivated the leaders to pursue leadership roles included the following: being "tapped on the shoulder," a desire to ensure high expectations, or, stated as the opposite, eradicating low expectations for students; contributing their linguistic capital; advocacy; and increased representation. Leaders expressed more than one motivation for their pursuit of leadership. This reveals that making such a decision to "leave the classroom," as it is often mentioned in schools, for leadership is often multifaceted, consisting of internal and external motivations.

ROUTES TAKEN TO LEADERSHIP

George's route to leadership began due to what he remembered as more than "a tap" on the shoulder. Perhaps it could be characterized as more of a "push."

He started his recollection about how he got into leadership by saying, "I didn't decide to go into administration. I was pretty much forced into it." He continued:

> I was a Special Ed teacher and a department chair. I loved teaching at a school out in California. I enjoyed it. The day before school started, I was doing interviews at the district office and there was a knock on the door. The secretary for the superintendent [said], "George, we need to see you in the superintendent's office." I finished up that interview and I'm thinking to myself, "What did I do? I'm in trouble." When I walked into the superintendent's office, the board president was sitting in there.
>
>   The principal was sitting in there with a few other people. And I sat down and they said, "Last night, there was an issue that occurred." The principal at an elementary school, the night before, was found passed out at a drive-through [restaurant] and he had drugs and alcohol in his car and he was being fired. They were gonna move the assistant principal of my middle school to that elementary school, and they were gonna name me the interim assistant principal. And I said, I didn't want it, and they say, "Well, there's no choices. You're going to be the interim assistant principal." And so I was an interim assistant principal.

George clarified that they did not actually force him, but strongly pressured him. He said they told him, "We really want you to do this. Will you do this?" After a while, he said, "Alright. Fine." He was an interim for about three months before he got a call from the superintendent again:

> I drive down, I figured, oh they're gonna try to talk me into taking the principal's job, or the assistant principal's job. Take the interim title off. I was actually having fun doing it so I was thinking, Yeah, I might do this, I think this would be cool. Now when I got to the superintendent's office, it was just him and the board president. And they said, "We're firing the principal and we're gonna name you the principal." And I said, "Wait, I've only been the assistant principal for three months." And they said, "Yes, but we have confidence." And so I became a principal.

Martha's path to the principalship was less forced. Her teaching career began in what she described as "three very distinct places"—Portland, Oregon; New Delhi, India; and WSD, where she was a bilingual resource teacher. That position required she have a bilingual license, which she did not have. Even though she had degrees in Spanish and elementary education, she had to go back to school. That led to an epiphany. She remembered:

> And then I decided at that point, that if I was gonna go back to school that wasn't where I was real passionate in terms of teaching. I didn't see myself

as a bilingual educator. So, I started those courses, but then I simultaneously enrolled in a doctorate program to push myself.

Martina and George served as mentors during Martha's field experiences as part of her doctoral program. She was encouraged to apply in WSD, and was hired as a principal.

The educational route to principal credentials was also a consideration for Cecilia. When she decided to pursue administration, she already held a master's degree in Reading. However, she explained, "I knew that if I wanted to be a principal I needed to have leadership." She was not interested in obtaining another master's degree so she completed the principal license.

Enrique held several different positions en route to becoming an administrator. He started off as a bilingual teacher's aide in a first-grade classroom. Then in consecutive order, he became an athletic coach, elementary school teacher, then "a parent and community involvement resource teacher, working with the parents in the community, creating environments conducive to them to their empowerment." He also taught summer enrichment programs. Next, he became an assistant principal, then elementary school principal, middle school principal, then high school principal. He noted, "that all happened within a span of fourteen years, the principalships. I was a middle school principal and then the Board of Education decided to send me to the largest high school, I was the youngest principal at the time."

Most of the school leaders started their careers in bilingual education. Enrique began as a bilingual teacher's aid. Antonio was a bilingual teacher in his first role, as was Martina. Sonia's first role was as a bilingual elementary education teacher, then literacy coach, and ultimately associate superintendent. Martina started her education career as a bilingual middle, then high school math teacher. She transitioned to a district-wide support teacher, completed a master's degree in educational administration, then became a coordinator. school principal, then executive director. Velma's "entire career has been in bilingual education." She was a bilingual teacher, principal of a school where the majority of students were of Dominican descent, just like her; then she became an elementary school superintendent. In general, these career trajectories follow the traditional paths from teacher, whether in bilingual or general education, to superintendent. Insight into leaders' motivations and career pathways to leadership have implications for those positioned to scaffold entry and progression into school leadership.

CONTENT QUESTION

• What was/is your inspiration for pursuing school leadership? How is your personal narrative similar or different to the school leaders' experiences?

REFLECTION QUESTIONS FOR LEARNING
FROM THE EXPERIENCES OF LATINA/O/X
ADMINISTRATORS: ENGRAVING

1. Consider the concept "tapping on the shoulder." Have you engaged in this informal type of encouragement for someone you know to enter leadership?
   a. Who do you or have you tapped on the shoulder? Have any of them been people who were of different identities than you? Were any Latina/o/x?
   b. How can you engage with Latina/o/x educators in or outside of your district to get to know them and include them in your network of potential people to be "tapped"?
2. Reflect on your beliefs about Latina/o/x bilingual educators. Have you consciously or subconsciously limited them to a particular role (sometimes referred to as pigeonholing)? How can you reset your assumptions to view them with potential to serve as leaders in a wide range of educational contexts?
3. What are some initial steps you might take to create pipeline programs, mentoring, or affinity groups for Latina/o/x school leaders?

Chapter 5

Social Justice Advocacy

Evidence from Latina/o/x School Leaders

School leaders describe a range of social justice advocacy practices they engaged in, in their school and community contexts. We highlight the ways in which pride in their Latino identities, cultures, and heritage informed their leadership approach. We also identify their advocacy for Latina/o/x students and families in particular.

EMBRACING THEIR LATINO HERITAGES

Cecilia: I love being a Hispanic, I love being a Latina, I love our culture.
Velma: I feel so lucky that I have the richness of my language and my culture at my fingertips. And that every summer, going back and forth to Dominican Republic, really solidified that.

Each administrators' leadership was informed by their knowledge, appreciation, and celebration of their cultural identities and heritages. While this may seem obvious, given the ways in which many educational systems marginalize Latino cultures and the Spanish language, it is important to note that their cultural appreciation was not diminished as they gained experience in the U.S. education system. In fact, Enrique and Antonio discussed how their cultural identity strengthened over time, which in turn, strengthened their leadership purpose and practices.

Identity-Consciousness and Power

Enrique: I think that one of the underlying realities that we deal with both in and outside of schools, is access to power. Access to resources that would allow us to, not necessarily put others down, but to lift ourselves up. And so, I've come to the conclusion, especially in this last several years, that power isn't going to be shared. You're going to have to grab it, you're gonna have to go for it. And then decide how you use it in an ethical and all-encompassing manner. I think this, the last four years especially [since President Trump was elected in 2016], have proven that we can make all the strides in the world and in one swoop, the system will take it back. And so I think we have to learn how to play a little bit more offense, and less defense. And I think our leadership approaches keep that in mind, that this is about giving people access, and giving people a fair opportunity to better their lives and in the process, better the lives of others.

Enrique made meaning of his purpose through his commitment to a collective Latino identity and the imperative to gain access to power for resources and decision-making. He continued:

I think that because of the struggles . . . because I might be considered a person of color, but I grew up with some economic advantages after my dad [became] a civil engineer. Before that we struggled but I am not gonna claim that we had it as hard as others do. We never went homeless. We never went a night without eating. So there's a lot of things that I've experienced, that have made me sort of reexamine my identity about who I am, and what I'm here to do. But I think that when it comes to those experiences, it lends itself to this idea of leadership being about going after the things that will give us the resources to live a full life; while at the same time not becoming the oppressor. So I think leadership is about understanding power dynamics, knowing how to ethically challenge those power dynamics, and then creating a space for you to be able to use that power to do more good than bad.

Enrique explained how aspects of his shared identity inform his sense of community with Latinx students, while also not over-generalizing his experiences.

Antonio also thought about his Latino heritage from a collective, although slightly different perspective:

Within our culture there's a resentment toward the Hispanic term, because it indicates that we came from Spain, versus Latin America which is Latino, we're all part of Latin America. I don't have a preference of one over the other, I think it's just a term. Like I said, I don't focus on the terms or even categorize myself as a strict Latino or a strict Mexican. It's just I feel like because of the way that I was raised, and the community I was raised [in], I feel like I kind of have a little bit of each culture, if that makes any sense. I don't strictly follow what the Mexican culture does, I don't strictly follow what Hispanics do. It's more of an embodiment of the people I've been around, if that makes sense.

Antonio's conceptualization of identity pushes the boundaries of what identity and culture mean. He attributed that to his experience growing up in the ethnically diverse Logan Square neighborhood in Chicago.

Identity, Representation, and Advocacy

Cecilia: I think if we represent at the table and leadership, if we represent the students that we represent, or the students that we support in our district, there's just more advocacy for our kids, right? You have to be able to understand and identify with the students you serve, if you really want to have their best interests at heart. So when I look around the room, and I'm the only Hispanic at the table, if I don't raise my voice, if I don't speak out, no one else is gonna speak up for them.

Cecilia expounded on why representation matters in material ways. She asserted:

We need to be at the table. We need to be having the conversation. We can't allow others who don't identify with our population or with our culture, or with our students to make decisions, which may not truly benefit our kids. So we need to have representation at the table for our Latino students, our Black students, every other student. And not just Latino because of the race, but languages, you know, our Haitian students, our Portuguese speaking students. Just our ELLs in general, regardless of where they're from. I can speak from the Hispanic point of view, but I can also speak from the ELL point of view, which will then encompass more cultures and other groups of students. So, yes, I think it's important that we continue to grow a diverse group of leaders.

Cecilia thought about her identity in terms of representation. Her thinking went beyond mere numeric representation of Latinos, to the implications of what increased representation in leadership means for addressing Latina/o/x students' and families' needs.

Indeed, diversity representation should go beyond numbers. When the right people are hired, counting them as leaders is important. Velma recalled the importance of her being visibly accounted for. The significance of her appointment as the principal of a mostly Dominican school to students, staff, and families was evident by their sheer surprise that she was the principal. She expounded:

I know, because of the feedback that I received from my families, I was the first Dominican principal they'd ever met. And that was huge, especially in [my city]. So just who I am, and who I bring absolutely influenced my practice. I think more importantly, the reflection of who I was from the community was very specific. Like even [families] walking in and looking around to look for the

principal. And I'd be like, "*Soy yo*" (I am). [They would respond], "Oh, okay."
I would get that, at least the first few years, all the time.

That phenomenon continued past her time as principal. She explained the
shock and gratitude she receives when other Dominicans realize she is an
administrator:

> Even now, as an elementary superintendent, I'll go visit my schools, and we
> often go through the cafeteria. And just the other day, *la señora Dominicana* (a
> Dominican woman) is the cafeteria manager, and the cafeteria managers tend to
> be *Dominicanas* in a lot of the schools, and they will literally stop and be like,
> "*Tu era Dominicana*" (You are Dominican)! And then I get that thing again, "*Y
> tu la jefa de mi jefa*" (You are the boss of my boss)! They're just, like, blown
> away that I'm now the boss of their principal. So, it humbles me. It's like, you
> take it for granted, you know, because you're doing the work.

HIGH ACADEMIC EXPECTATIONS

Antonio: I do feel strongly about having high expectations because I know that
I came from a community that struggled and had very limited resources, but I
was able to do it because I had expectations for myself, my parents had high
expectations, and I feel that's something that's needed at the school level.

Antonio theorized one possible reason for the prevalence of low expectations
in schools is because poor students and Latinx students "do not have as much
resources, [so] other cultures think that 'we're gonna coddle or we're gonna
water down instruction to help these kids out.'" Instead, he believed "it's
really about having those high expectations and having those supports, to
really help students be successful." Further, he clarified that his commitment
to upholding high expectations extends to all students. He asserted, " I don't
really see it as I'm just impacting Hispanics. I see it as I'm impacting kids
of color and kids that are low income, because that's what I identify myself
with."

Similarly, George explained why he believes it is important that students
have access to diverse representations of role models who are examples of
what they can achieve. He used his own experience as motivation, as he
recalled how he did not have Latino role models in school. However, there
was a coach who took him "under his wing."

Antonio and George expressed their commitment to maintaining high
expectations for students as a result of their experiences as students. They
viewed high expectations as essential for creating a school culture that is

undergirded by a belief in the potential of all students to excel. In our view, a commitment to high expectations is one of the most important actions of social justice leaders because enacting high expectations is a direct disruption of deficit thinking. All of our leaders expressed this commitment in one way or another. We highlight excerpts of their *testimonios* to underscore this point.

Antonio: High expectations, that's a big one for me. Really understanding and knowing that all kids are capable if we have the right scaffolds and support that they need.

Cecilia: It's our job as educators to inform [students] throughout middle school and high school of what [post-secondary education] looks like, help them apply to college, help them find scholarships. Because the parents at home, they want it. They want what's best for their children.

Enrique: I told someone the other day that our system wasn't designed for the kids that we serve. Our system was never designed for low income, like Latinx, African American kids to make it. And so our job is to redesign the system, so that these kids do have an opportunity. And that's what I enjoy doing. So whenever a kid that wasn't supposed to make it, makes it, I get happy.

George: I need kids to see that you can do all these other things and you can do it 'cause I could do it. And we can sit down and try to support you to get there.

Martha: I feel like our Latino families feel very connected to school, more than other places, more than any other school I've been at.

Martina: I think we know from the current status quo that education does work for, say, language-majority White families. It's working and we have data that show that. So I think we still have to work [to answer], What are the current excellent pedagogies that lead to excellence for [all] students? We still need to implement that.

Sonia: Dual language learners are an asset to our city, to our country. Immigrants are, too. I would love my legacy [to be] that every child graduates bilingual.

Velma: When I became an administrator, as a principal, as a school superintendent, my number one duty is to do right by families; and to do right by them is to understand what their goals are for their children, and to help them reach those goals, whatever those are. Not to make assumptions about anything.

HONORING AND UPHOLDING BILINGUALISM

Bilingualism (linguistic capital) is an important asset for most of the leaders as they create welcoming environments for Spanish-speaking families. This was accomplished by eliminating the language barriers that exist when a family's home language is not English.

Although Martha did not grow up speaking Spanish, she learned it as an adult. Martha credits the Spanish dual language immersion (DLI) program for centering Spanish as a dominant language in her school. Families are comfortable speaking their home language in the school. She explained:

> I think that the DLI program takes care of a lot of it. So it breaks down language barriers with teachers and families, and I think that communication can be one of the biggest hurdles to overcome. So whether it's a potluck or it's coming in for a celebration, they know that their language is privileged in the school.

Velma understood that speaking and listening to families who spoke Spanish increased their voice. She wondered, "How do you know that you have voice if you never see anyone that understands you?" To increase access to families, she "did a lot of translating at IEP meetings, because sometimes the folks that were sent to translate were terrible." An IEP is an Individualized Education Program designed for students who receive special education. Schools are required to hold an annual meeting which includes parents/caregivers, to review students' IEPs. Since these meetings review the educational services students receive, it is important that parents understand the language of the IEP itself and the language used by educators during the meeting. Velma's questions are extremely important, especially in this context, since comprehension and communication have specific implications regarding the parents/caregiver's ability to advocate for their children and ask questions about services. She pondered, "What does it mean to have voice? To me, this question is about whose voice represents who."

In other aspects of schooling, Velma worked to ensure the voices of her community were included by celebrating their stories and experiences. Underscoring the urgency of dismantling deficit-thinking, she emphasized it is important to have "a narrative that's not about the deficit of our community. Rather, it's the celebration of we have some incredible people in our community that live and breathe and demonstrate culturally and linguistically, all of the things that we love." Velma also compared her efforts to include the cultural and linguistic diversity of her families to her own experience in schools. She remembered,

> But that didn't exist in my schools. In my schooling, I had to choose between learning English because I entered school Spanish dominant. And, I remember specifically being told to speak only English. So for many years, I was silent in school. So for me, my work is about how do I never allow that silence.

As she reflected on her strengths as an administrator, Martina expounded on the importance of multilingualism. She explained,

I think bilingualism and multilingualism is a concrete way that has opened doors for me to connect with people of different backgrounds, directly. I think a monolingual principal has to rely on an interpreter all the time, and usually the interpreter becomes the broker and sometimes the power conduit. The communication can stop with the interpreter, if the interpreter doesn't realize what power they have, and sometimes they can stop the conversation being an asset of the principal and kind of take over . . . and the communication ends with the interpreter. So in my case, what I saw then, was that many families were being cut off from direct access to the decision makers and the people who have the broad view. And that's a shortcoming then for the principal that's monolingual, when they give up the power, and the power to listen actually, to parents, to the interpreter.

Martina recognized her multilingualism as linguistic capital because it allowed her to directly connect with families. In contrast, monolingual leaders required an interpreter. She went further, by analyzing how language and access to power (the principal) in terms of decision-making have material consequences for families.

Antonio, who is a bilingual Spanish speaker, built relationships with families and was able to avoid the challenges Martina described above. He made it a point to tell families that they could talk directly to him, rather than relying on an interpreter. He recounted, "I basically made it very clear, 'You can always talk directly to me. There's not a language barrier, you can talk to me.'"

Enrique's goal is to transform the ways that English language learners are fundamentally viewed. He declared:

I'm trying to start a movement where we stop calling them ELLs and we call them HTBs, halfway to bilingual versus English language learner. I think that we live in a world, that due to reasons that I think more are in line with people's interpretation of immigration, do not see bilingualism as an asset, when that's exactly what it is. You ask any White middle class, upper middle class parent that's monolingual, "Do you want your kids to be bilingual?" They'll tell you, "Absolutely." Because they know that within the context of a global economy, that means assets, that means power, that means economic security. So we have kids coming in with a language already, and more than enough knowledge to add another one. Why aren't we doing it? I think it's more indicative of people's biases becoming action than being common sensical about the fact that this is simply an asset versus a deficit.

Enrique's thoughts about language exemplify his belief that learning languages is an asset, and that eliminating deficit views about Latino families learning English is essential. His hope is that society at large, will shift toward recognizing bi- and multilingualism as assets. Also, like Martina, he recognizes the ways in which economic status, language, and power converge to create narratives about what is considered a deficit or asset in our society.

Centering Race, Culture, and Language in Institutional Changes and Decision-Making

As the central office administrator in charge of multilingual and global education, Martina ensured the needs of English language learners were included in plans for assessing special education and gifted programming. She sought to create a systemic focus on academic supports for the inclusion of Latina/o/x students in honors and gifted courses. She recognized:

> There are still a lot of the people that work in those departments, that mostly understand their fields for monolingual students, but they don't necessarily understand bilingual students. So at this point I still try to bring awareness that, "Really it's your department that really should be developing the expertise, but until that happens let's engage in a dialogue and we can help you learn about that."

Martina's efforts required constant conversations based on relationship-building and trust. She balanced "advocacy and the sharing of information" while advocating for a system-wide ownership of providing services for Latina/o/x students and English language learners. This was particularly challenging in a district that hired leaders of special education and gifted programs that lacked knowledge of English language learners.

Principals Martha, Antonio, and George explained their role in facilitating difficult conversations about race, privilege, bias, and inequity. Martha credited the district for providing a framework:

> The district's been working with [a national organization], and there's a big push to talk about equity. We've done some work with implicit bias, but really unpacking that for ourselves, and trying to get to a spot where all parties involved feel comfortable talking about race, which is not really ever the case, actually.

Antonio opined that the most effective aspect of race and equity work is building trusting relationships with staff. He invested in

> trying to help staff build a deeper understanding of the identities in front of them. Some of them have to do with race and equity work, like building those relationships, not only with students but with families, and really helping to identify "what are these students bringing with them?" I think being that I was a first-year principal, I think it's the initial startup . . . peeling those underlying deeper issues that have come out that really solidify that people do not feel like kids of color are ready to have certain learning experiences or are ready to learn. It's been a lot of work around getting people to really understand what are some implicit biases that they're coming with.

As a first-year principal, he recognized the importance of developing trust trust in order to lean into the discomfort that often accompanies discussions about diversity.

George took a different, seemingly more direct approach to discussions about race and equity during his first year as high school principal. This is, likely because unlike Antonio and Martha, who were in their first and second years as head principals, his first year at the high school came after fourteen years as a principal in various middle schools. He reflected:

> I know that I don't care about having friends. I have friends, right? I'm willing to have that tough conversation. I'm willing to have the culturally-based conversations and ask those questions of why historically, it's been allowed to happen and why, in the future, we're gonna continue to [eliminate] some practices that I feel are both racist as well as just plain stupid. And I have ruffled a lot of feathers this past year because I've asked these questions and continue to say, "And why are we still doing this if these are the results?" And there's only so much we can keep pointing and saying "it's the kids" when [there are only] two variables—the adult and the practice.

Enrique shared a *testimonio* about the challenges that can arise when people perceive that hiring practices result in changing demographics, without unpacking their previous assumptions. He shared,

> Understanding that I now had positional authority, in addition to personal authority; and using that combination to change aspects of the system that I believe were actually designed to keep certain children from my community down, I began to hire people that were more in line with this idea about redesigning a system so that children of all backgrounds could benefit, especially children that came from [my background]. I learned quickly that when you start doing that, people are gonna start going after you. They're gonna start questioning, why is he hiring those people? I can hire twenty-three White people, and no one's gonna say a word. But I hire, you know, six Latinos, seven African Americans, and the rest White, and people are like, "That's a lot of Latino [and] Black folks that you hired," right? So, I had to learn how to play the game.

In response, Enrique developed strategies so that he could achieve his goals while maintaining professional relationships with different stakeholders. He continued:

> I could have gone in, you know, and just said, "I'm gonna do it," and then when they fire me, [say] "screw it." But I wanted to sustain as much of my existence as possible. So that means ethically, learning how to play the game. So not everyone has to go to a board meeting. But I'm gonna go to all the board meetings,

because if I get to know those people, and they get to know me, they'll see that I'm trying to do good. So creating social capital between members of the Board of Education and myself.

Martina centered race and ethnicity when thinking about diversity and representation in books. As a principal, she focused on

broadening the types of books that are available in schools. I think those are areas that between the librarians and the classroom teachers you can do. What we had to work on more was broadening the concept of what are different Latino groups that were represented. Not only the Mexican-American experience, but other subgroups within Latinos. Afro-Latinos, Latinos from South America, their immigration experience. And so having a broad range of, "What does it mean to be Latino in the US?"

Race, culture, and language consciousness, developed within the school leaders for the most part, since youth, influenced how they have evaluated policies and institutional structures, and engaged in decision-making. They were committed to these discussions as essential parts of their work.

PARENT AND FAMILY ENGAGEMENT: WORKING ALONGSIDE PARENTS/FAMILIES

School leaders centered race and culture, and included multiple voices in decision-making in their approaches to parent/family engagement. Their visions of family involvement transcended traditional notions of parents being present during the school day to help with school activities. They created systems that engaged parents to influence school systems or use institutional knowledge to make decisions that best fit their students' needs.

The leaders underscored their commitment to learning from families. For example, Cecilia described her general approach as, "I try to understand what their needs are, where they're coming from, so that we can better serve them. Because to me, it's not, you hold a leadership position and you are in charge." This reflects her disavowal of a perspective that leadership is purely hierarchical.

Sonia understood that parents want to know how their children are doing in school. They might ask, "*Como se portan* (How are the kids behaving)?" She encouraged creative ways for parents to engage in learning with their children, such as parent workshops where the parents wrote books about their life as a child and read them to children.

Another important characteristic of family engagement was the leaders' work alongside parents rather than as experts who assumed the parents needed to be told what to do. Velma narrated her transformation toward this practice early in her teaching career:

> I would say that that was the biggest lesson for me as a teacher and as a principal. How I had to learn what it meant to be co-conspirators in the work. I think in the beginning, I was trained very traditionally, like most teacher programs, where you send out information. Oh, *su hija hi* (your daughter) didn't bring her homework. It took time, and I will say, quickly, I was humbled very fast. Especially in the community where I taught, that wasn't enough. That wasn't going to give me any results. And that if I didn't figure out it's not the mom that I call, it's actually the *tia* (aunt). And they don't live with their dad, they actually live with the grandmother. I had to figure out the complexity of our community's actual network. And specifically, [the] network of support for their children.

This was not hard for Velma to understand because she processed what was happening in the context of her own upbringing. She recognized "that it was just as complex, if not more complex in my own upbringing. Because we always had an *abuela* (grandmother) or *tio* (uncle) or somebody in the house, helping with the kids." Notably, she shifted her thinking about what was considered normal based on her personal story. She continued, "That was normal. And my knowledge of that absolutely helped me think about how to include Latino families [in a way that] was almost the antithesis of what I was taught in the teacher program."

Velma emphasized the importance of her situating herself as a learner of her families, even though she came from a similar background. She said:

> I feel really lucky to have learned. Those ten years as the principal took it to even a different level of learning. Like my even assuming, just because I'm Dominican, I have a similar story to the person in front of me who's Dominican, too? *Para nada* (Not at all). Really always being open to that lesson of what is unique about this family that I'm speaking to right now, that's gonna help me move the academic goals and the hopes and dreams of that family for that student that I am serving.

She reiterated that learning about the families and communities she serves is "ever-evolving" and requires always learning how to do it better and better. To emphasize the importance of ongoing learning, Velma stated, "And I hope the day that I say 'I know how to do it,' is the day I retire."

Enrique explained how he listened to and learned from parents and incorporated their questions, feedback, and experiences into his decision-making. For example, he said, "the fact that we created an English learner task force. Because what good is saying we have to improve learning for our ELs, if we don't have a team behind that?" As another example, he shared, "When families came forward and said, 'we really appreciate all your emphasis on college, but we don't know what that is. We've never been to one.'" In response, the school arranged parent university tours.

Martha facilitated opportunities for parents to ask questions and determine if the dual language immersion program was the right fit for their students, rather than automatically placing Latino students in the DLI program. She stated, "I think that by trying to convince them [to only consider DLI], I'm taking away the power that they have to make decisions for their families."

Martina identified two practices she implemented as a school principal that engaged parents equitably. First, she provided parents with information they used to advocate for themselves. Sometimes those parents advocated for Latinx families in other schools that did not offer the same opportunity for Latinx parent/caregiver empowerment. When she was a principal, Martina offered "specific training on leadership for parents through the MALDEF, Mexican American Legal Defense Fund curriculum." The curriculum teaches parents about how school systems work and how they can become active participants in school processes. She noticed that families who attended her school and received the training, then moved to another school where the training and support for parents did not occur, did not want to settle for less. She reflected:

> Then they start standing up and they start demanding, "Can we have a meeting for Latino parents? Can we have a potluck for ELLs, for Latinos?" And so they are also becoming agents of change in other schools which is exactly what we need. It's also slowly affecting and improving our district as a whole.

This example demonstrates how information and education, when presented with the intent to address the needs of parents based on their perspectives, elevates their involvement.

Second, Martina narrated lessons she learned when she was a principal of a dual language immersion elementary school:

> What happened was the issue of homework. It was so interesting because the parents, all the parents were telling us, "This whole thing with homework is not working out." So we had a meeting with parents of different grade levels and the feedback that we got was very actually stunning when we understood it. A lot of our Anglo parents in the dual language program, so very supportive of their children becoming bilingual, would tell us, "We don't want you assigning homework to our kids because our kids are enrolled in swimming, soccer, piano, violin after school. I don't have time for homework. They don't have time for homework, I don't have time to supervise." And our Latino parents, our Latino moms would come out with the opposite saying, "We want homework. We want our kids to

know their math facts. I want them to do their worksheets every night. I make a point of staying home so that I can support it. We want homework."

And the teachers and I were dumbfounded that parents were requesting the exact opposite. And it was pretty much by ethnic, cultural, language groups as the divide. And so we had to go back as a school team and decide one, what was our collective position around the issue of homework, because we were all over the place. Each teacher would have a different practice depending on their own personal belief and as a school we didn't have sort of a vision or a policy around that. So in this case, the parents did influence us to do something different in our practices. And as a matter of fact, the only way that we reinstituted this as a school-wide practice was [the creation of a universal homework policy that said] "This many minutes of reading per grade level." That was universal for everybody.

And homework, we decided that, one, it had to be at the independent level so kids were not learning something new for homework. Maybe they had to teach it to parents and needed to show what they could do, but it wasn't something that the parents obviously had to teach the child. And then parents would sign up, "I want homework." Or, "I don't homework." And depending on that, the teachers put the homework in the folders for each student. And so they [parents] actually did influence our practice through that.

Martina's *testimonio* reveals the potential for providing equitable supports for students when culturally responsive leaders listen to and include diverse parents and perspectives in decision-making. As evidenced in Martina's experience, leaders must also develop the skills to navigate conflict resolution.

In this chapter, we've identified several mindsets and actions Latina/o/x school leaders employed to advocate for equity, access for Latina/o/x students and families. Advocacy actions included embracing their race and ethnic identity as part of their leadership identity; supporting high academic expectations for students; centering race and culture in institutional decision-making; and working alongside parents and caregivers, which starts with listening to and valuing their perspectives.

CONTENT QUESTIONS

- Which passages from school leaders' *testimonios* resonate the most with you, regarding dismantling deficit thinking and low expectations for Latina/o/x students and families?
- Which passages resonate the most with you, regarding upholding high expectations for Latina/o/x students and families?
- What aspects of leader's beliefs and practices for engaging families are priorities for you to incorporate into your leadership practice?

REFLECTION QUESTION FOR LEARNING
FROM THE EXPERIENCES OF LATINA/O/X
ADMINISTRATORS: ENGRAVING

Velma remembered that she stayed silent in school for years, because she was a Spanish-dominant speaker in English-dominant schools. Now, as a leader, her work is about how she "will never allow that silence." After learning about the importance of uplifting bilingualism in schools, what programs, policies, and practices will you support to ensure that as a leader, you, too, "will never allow that silence" of bilingual students and families?

Chapter 6

Latino Educational Leadership

We connect the *testimonios* of the Latina/o/x school leaders to the construct of Latino Educational Leadership (Rodríguez et al., 2018). Then, we draw connections between the *testimonios*, constructs we discussed in chapter 1 (anti-deficit-based thinking, critical race theory, LatCrit, community cultural wealth, social justice leadership and advocacy, culturally responsive school leadership), and Latino Educational Leadership (LEL).

According to Rodriguez et al., "Latino Educational Leadership in K-12 settings must foster democratic, inclusive, and collaborative educational practices . . . with school and district leaders who are willing to engage in activist practices alongside Latino families to combat educational, cultural, and social oppression" (p. 8). The Latina/o/x leaders exhibited five leadership characteristics which are reflected in existing scholarship about Latina/o/x leaders and align with LEL. They are (1) embracing a collective Latino identity, or *Latinidad*; (2) acknowledging forms of community cultural wealth in their life histories and expecting to find it within their students and families; (3) focusing on linguistic capital as they advocate for bilingualism in schools; (4) equitable family and community engagement; and (5) social justice advocacy.

EMBRACING A COLLECTIVE LATINO IDENTITY: *LATINIDAD*

Velma: When you talk about the importance of educating Latinos, it's, I hope I honor my community by doing what I do, you know? And just being myself and loving my people. Just loving them.

Cultural, racial, and ethnic heritage identities are important to the Latina/o/x leaders whose personal and professional lives are centered in this book. Velma explained that this sense of collective identity among Latinos is how she is able to connect with others by celebrating her identity. She commented, "It's interesting that that comes from my *Latinidad* (being a Latino), and my connection with my *Latinidad* and how I connect that to my actual work."

Latinidad refers to the collective identity of Latina/o/x peoples whose countries of origin are the Spanish-speaking countries of Central America, South America, and the Caribbean islands (San Miguel, 2011). San Miguel noted, "Each Latino group is distinct in its own way, but it is also part of larger historical, political, and cultural processes affecting all racialized minority groups in the country" (pp. 9–10). As leaders discussed their identity and leadership, they demonstrated their commitment to both dimensions of *Latinidad*. They seamlessly discussed their own cultural group and heritage when reflecting on their personal experience, and pivoted to a discussion of Latinos in general when thinking about what experiences and characteristics bind them together. Three ways *Latinidad* informed leadership practices were (a) acknowledging identity; (b) connecting to and understanding students and families through shared experiences; and (c) accepting the significance of their representation in leadership as role models and symbols of success by the Latino community.

Honoring and Celebrating Identity

Sonia, as did several other leaders, discussed larger themes among Latinos, which she connected to her personal family history. Her ability to think collectively and individually at the same time supports her to think broadly about Latina/o/x students and families, without ignoring nuances within and between individuals and ethnic groups. Sonia reflected, "I think we are family oriented. [We think about what is] good for the group, which is counter to American culture [and its focus on] competition, which is not always desirable." She continued to discuss the strength she derives from Mexican history and the struggles Mexicans have endured. Sonia pointed out that other cultures have tried to conquer Mexico but asserted, "*soy peleonera* (I am a fighter). In my culture we have female icons . . . *Las adelitas* (women who took up arms to fight for independence)." Her sense of history is strong because, she explained, "my father is a history buff so we learned a lot of history." Both of her parents have a "second grade education." They made sure Sonia learned about the role of women in history. For example, she read books by Juana Ines de la Cruz, a famous Mexican author. She describes her family as "open and book smart, open to discussions" because "it's common in Latin America to talk about politics."

The way that Sonia's family, ethnic, and Latino identity informs her approach to education is indicative of the ways other Latina/o/x leaders made sense of their heritage, family, and leadership. This understanding rooted in her heritage is important because it disrupts school discourses that normalize the avoidance of Latino race, ethnicity, or culture. Although Latinos as a group is comprised of multiple races and ethnicities, the importance of honoring identity applies to the collective Latino experience.

Shared Experience

Cecilia recounted experiences navigating homework and applying for college. Her parents were supportive of her doing well in school. Because her parents were not fluent in English, Cecilia figured out how to complete homework and she applied for college on her own. As a result, she can relate to what ELLs go through today. Her shared experience informs her leadership perspective. She understands that the language barriers parents face are not deficits which are indicative of a lack of interest or high expectations.

Cecilia discussed the distinction between her expertise gained because of her personal and institutional experiences. She said, "When [people say] 'Oh, my God, Cecilia, you're just so knowledgeable,' [I think to myself,] "I'm knowledgeable because I have institutional knowledge. I've been an educator for thirty-three years. I have institutional knowledge [and] personal experience that I bring to the table."

Role Models/Representation

Similar to the pride and surprise members of the Dominican community bestowed upon Cecilia when they realized she was a school leader, Sonia described how her presence as a Latina leader made her a role model for other Latinas: "A lot of women are coming to me, saying, 'We are so glad to see a Latina at your level.' They tell me I am a role model and that Latinas can be leaders." Because Sonia revived dual language programs, which reduces the trajectory for ELLs placed in separate educational programs, she is seen as an advocate and a role model within her community.

Crawford and Fuller (2017) contended that although there is little, if any, evidence that demonstrates a direct link between the race or ethnicity of a principal and student outcomes, historically marginalized groups such as Latinos benefit directly and indirectly from having principals of color. Representational bureaucracy occurs when "the characteristics of a public official [in this case, Latina/o/x educational leaders] mimic the characteristics of a population she represents" (p. 1172). The more the leader's characteristics match the population, the more likely the leader will make decisions and enact policy that benefit the group. Benefits for Latina/o/x communities have been found to be more adoption of school policies considered beneficial to Latino students. Other benefits include principals' service as role models, which shapes positive identity development and positive student outcomes in achievement, course selection, and school discipline (Crawford & Fuller, 2017; Sanchez et al., 2008).

COMMUNITY CULTURAL WEALTH

We focused on three forms of community cultural wealth that emerged from the leaders' *testimonios*: aspirational, familial, and linguistic. They described how their personal and educational experiences contributed to the development of these various forms of capital.

All of the leaders described how they were raised within a culture of high academic expectations, which developed aspirational capital that they used to motivate students and create cultures of high expectations in their schools. The leaders also recognized and valued their familial connections to immigration which shaped their empathy and understanding for families facing issues related to immigration. Additionally, linguistic capital was important. They honored home languages and advocated for Spanish to be centered in schools.

The school leaders' *testimonios* demonstrated, as previous scholars have identified, "the significant role that family background and racial identity play in shaping the trajectories of Latinx educational leaders" (Sampson, 2009, p. 317). Their experiences with racism and oppression created a critical lens through which the administrators addressed contemporary racial issues.

The lived experiences of Latina/o/x school leaders are important because first, they provide a counternarrative to deficit-laden untruths about Latina/o/x students and families. Yosso (2005) explained that the concept of cultural wealth "allows critical race scholars to 'see' multiple forms of cultural wealth within Communities of Color" (p. 82). The cultural wealth of the Latina/o/x school leaders in this study is a source of strength in their professional lives. Their community cultural wealth, which benefits schools, also reveals key assets that should be recognized in district and school hiring practices.

LINGUISTIC CAPITAL:
UPHOLDING BILINGUALISM WITHIN SCHOOLS

It is evident that the school leaders drew from their community cultural wealth to contextualize why advocacy is critical and how to go about it.

This was especially true as they upheld bilingualism as an asset within their schools. Sonia echoed the sentiments of other leaders such as Antonio, when she explained why she values bilingualism. She believes her legacy as an associate superintendent will be centered around bilingualism. First, she wants her community to know "that dual language learners are an asset to our city, to our country, [and] immigrants, too." Second, she professed, "I would love my legacy [to be] that every child graduates bilingual. As a school district, we will ensure that all kids graduate bilingual."

DeMatthews et al. (2017) explained it takes students several years to develop academic English proficiency. Teachers and principals require ongoing professional development and coaching to support Latina/o/x emergent bilinguals. They explained, "the role of the superintendent is therefore critical, given their positional authority to envision and make such investments at the district level" (p. 3). Their investigation of a Latino superintendent committed to the establishment of Spanish dual language education revealed many factors that are required for such advocacy. These included being mindful of the sociopolitical context of the school district, thinking critically about problems within the school district, acting courageously, and addressing state-level challenges such as the state's bilingual education certification policy.

ASSET-BASED FAMILY AND COMMUNITY ENGAGEMENT

The school leaders demonstrated their commitment to asset-based family engagement. This oriented their engagement with families as equals. Enrique and Velma articulated a key principle necessary for this, as they disavowed the notion that they were empowering families. Enrique said:

> I learned very quickly, that schools cannot empower children, but we can create environments conducive to their empowerment. Empowerment comes from within. We're giving ourselves too much credit when we say "I empowered him" or "I empowered her." I think it's much more powerful to create environments conducive to self-empowerment. And that's what I value as an educator still, thirty years later.

Velma continued by saying, "I find it patronizing to say, 'I'm empowering a community.' It's more about, what am I learning from the community? I'm the student. They're not the student." Enrique and Velma pointed out that they are not experts "giving" power to families who are operating from a deficit. Instead, they transform inequitable systems to create spaces where families can lean into self-empowerment. We understand there are researchers and activists who may use the term "empowerment" with the intention of acknowledging the ability and efficacy of Latino families to engage in self-advocacy. For example, Pstross et al.'s (2014) article "Empowering Latino parents to transform the education of their children" described the ways in which Latino parents are involved in college preparation of their K-12 students. The researchers studied how a program called "The American Dream Academy" helped Latino families overcome barriers to the college planning process. They begin their article by asserting, "Helping parents to empower themselves with the necessary knowledge and skills to frame the education of their child can have a transformative impact on the future of that child" (p. 650). In one way, the term "empower" in this context could be viewed as educating ignorant families. From a different perspective, the education offered in the program is designed to promote equitable engagement and information to navigate school systems, thereby contributing to "self-empowerment." These nuances reveal the importance of language and the context in which it is used.

Asset-based family engagement requires leaders to work alongside families, to value who they are, and recognize their expertise. The leaders engaged in asset-based inquiry. They learned formally and informally from students and families about how they engage with schools. Velma shared an example of how she has developed the skills to be a student of the deaf community that she serves - a community that is not her own. Referencing how much she has learned, she explained," that has helped and sustained me, as I work with the deaf community, which is not my community. So I bring that knowledge of being a student of the community to other communities that are not as familiar to me." Velma transfers her commitment to asset-based learning as well as the skills she has acquired, to other communities.

SOCIAL JUSTICE ADVOCACY

Advocacy for students and families is central to the paradigm of social justice (Hernandez et al., 2014) and Latino Educational Leadership. It was central to the leaders profiled here. At its core, this type of social justice advocacy requires leaders who serve Latina/o/x communities to navigate institutions and systems "to improve educational opportunity and equity for diverse learners" (Rodríguez et al., 2016, p. 148). This was reiterated by Martinez et al. (2016) who asserted that social justice advocacy requires a commitment for developing relationships with all stakeholders (staff, faculty, and community) for the goal of transforming educational experiences of the students they serve.

Now, we review how the constructs described in this book are related. Figure 6.1 is a visual representation of how key constructs relate to each other and contribute to Latino Educational Leadership. The four boxes include characteristics that are essential to understanding each construct, along with references to key scholarship. Increasing scholarship continues to buttress what is known about each construct. We selected three or four resources that we considered to be seminal, are highly cited, and/or focus on Latina/o/x leaders, students, and families. They are not an exhaustive list of resources, by any means. We invite you to consider them as a starting point. The framework is intended to be read clockwise, starting at the top left box labeled Critical Race Theory & Lat Crit. The arrows between each construct represent our conceptualization of the general evolution of and relationships between constructs. For example, critical race theory informs critiques of deficit thinking; these constructs informed Yosso's development of community cultural wealth. Note, this is not an entirely chronological display of these constructs,

Critical Race Theory & LatCrit
(Bernal, 2002; Delgado & Stefancic, 2017; Ladson-Billings & Tate, 2005; Solórzano & Yosso, 2001)

Dismantle Deficit Thinking; Develop Asset-Based Thinking
(González et al., 2005; Valencia, 2010)

Community Cultural Wealth
(Rodela & Rodriguez-Mojica, 2019; Yosso, 2005)
Funds of knowledge - six forms of capital: aspirational, linguistic, familial, social, navigational, resistant

Latino Educational Leadership
(Martinez et al.,2016; Rodríguez et al., 2016; 2018)
Latinidad, self-reflection about community cultural wealth, Spanish bi- or multilingualism (linguistic capital); equitable family and community engagement; social justice advocacy (against oppression)
Critical Applied Leadership

Culturally Responsive School Leadership
(Gardiner & Enomoto, 2005; Khalifa et al., 2016)
Four behaviors: critical self-awareness; curriculum and teacher preparation; school environments; engaging students and parents in community contexts

Social Justice Leadership & Advocacy
(Dantley & Tillman, 2010; Kemp-Graham, 2015; Murakami et al., 2016; Theoharis, 2007)
-race, class, gender, language, and other historically marginalized identities are central to leadership vision and advocacy
-dismantles school inequities
-engages with families as equals
-high academic expectations

Figure 6.1   Framework of Constructs That Contribute to Latino Educational Leadership.

as key concepts within them continue to evolve. Concepts also overlap. For example, social justice leadership and advocacy, and culturally responsive share many concepts. Critical race theory, community cultural wealth, social justice leadership and advocacy, and culturally responsive leadership all include foundational concepts that inform Latino Educational Leadership.

CONTENT QUESTION

- In what ways does figure 6.1 help you make meaning of the key constructs that informed our understanding of Latina/o/x school leaders' *testimonios*?

Chapter 7

Promising Practices for Engraving
Latino Educational Leadership

We explore practices that (a) support the recruitment, retention, and inclusion of Latina/o/x school leaders by honoring their community cultural wealth and (b) identify beliefs and practices that can be incorporated into district practice so that the benefits of Latina/o/x leaders' culturally responsive practices can become engraved upon and throughout the district. In other words, so that Latina/o/x leaders may have influence on general district and school leadership practices in significant and enduring ways.

PRACTICES TO RECRUIT AND RETAIN
LATINA/O/X SCHOOL LEADERS

Cecilia: I can speak from the Hispanic point of view, but I can also speak from the ELL point of view, which will then encompass more cultures and other groups of students. So, yes, I think it's important that we continue to grow a diverse group of leaders.

We start with recruitment because engraving practices is a twofold endeavor. First, the hiring of more Latina/o/x leaders is important for Latina/o/x outcomes in schools. Second, school districts need to learn from best practices of culturally responsive Latina/o/x leaders so non-Latina/o/x leaders can build their capacity to enact culturally responsive, critical approaches to leadership that sustain Latina/o/x families and students' engagement and achievement.

Recruitment and Retention of Latina/o/x School Leaders

Rodela et al. (2019) explained how Latinx administrators in their study were recruited into roles because of their bilingualism. Current school and district leaders are in a position to identify the strengths of Latina/o/x leaders and encourage them by "tapping them on the shoulder" to ask if they have considered leadership or by encouraging them to apply for a position. In order for Latina/o/x faculty and staff to be considered, those in the position to do the "tapping" have to unpack any existing biases that prohibit them from seeing the strengths of Latina/o/x faculty and staff. This includes avoiding a tendency to pigeonhole Latina/o/x educators in bilingual educator roles. This is not to suggest that bilingual education is inferior to other education departments; rather, the choice and pathways for advancement should be left to the individual to pursue their interest and determine their career trajectory.

Encouragement such as "tapping on the shoulder" may lead to "sponsor mobility," where a senior administrator sponsors, endorses, or supports a junior administrator's career. This is why taking account of who is being "tapped" or "sponsored" is critical. If senior administrators do not purposely pay attention to the extent to which junior administrators they "sponsor" are diverse, the practice effectively excludes diverse candidates from being prepared for leadership. This is particularly true if the senior administrators are White and male, because they are more likely to sponsor someone who looks like them (Ortiz, 2001).

Same race mentoring for Latina/o/x administrators has promise for increasing their retention. Magdaleno (2006) designed a structured mentoring program that requires participants to meet a minimum of four times a year. Although Latina leaders identified mentors outside of their professional organizations as important, it is critical that formal networking and mentoring opportunities exist within professional spaces (Menchaca et al., 2017; Méndez-Morse, 2004).

Latina/o/x leaders may feel isolated or marginalized in their positions, particularly if they are the only one or one of a few. They may be asked to perform tasks or services that their non-Latina/o/x counterparts are not. For example, a Latina principal recounted how she was often asked to interpret for Spanish-speaking families in the district (Rodela et al., 2019). While we uphold bilingualism as an asset, this does not mean that Latina/o/x leaders should be burdened to take on duties outside the scope of their job expectations. If more interpreters are needed, districts should invest in attracting more Spanish-language interpreters. Another avenue, related to our concept of engraving, is if school leaders are asked to interpret for families, non-Latina/o/x leaders should be encouraged to become bilingual. Finally, to avoid the isolation that Latina school leaders feel once on the job, the creation of district-supported affinity groups may support this.

ENGRAVING BEST PRACTICES

Critically oriented leadership that embraces tenets of social justice advocacy on behalf of Latina/o/x students is not limited to Latina/o/x leaders or leaders of color. In other words, we agree with Rodríguez et al. (2018) that leaders of all races, ethnicities, and cultural backgrounds can (and should) develop their capacity to be social justice leaders in schools. Evidence of such leadership will be seen in schools that embrace, uplift, and create equitable access to enriching, relevant, engaging, and rigorous academic opportunities for Latina/o/x students and families. Of course, we realize that identity cannot be "engraved" upon those who do not identify as Latina/o/x. However, the development of asset-based understandings of the lived experiences, cultural identities, beliefs, and practices of Latina/o/x families can be achieved by all. Further, over-generalizations and stereotypes about Latina/o/x families will likely erode, as leaders get to know families individually. Family engagement skills can be learned by those outside of the Latina/o/x cultural community, if there is a willingness to learn. The ways in which Latina/o/x leaders make meaning of their leadership role, which often includes the perceived benefits of their leadership to community members who share their identity or "look like them," yields another promising practice for all school leaders. That is, to acknowledge the centrality of race, ethnicity, and culture. Latina/o/x heritages should not be disregarded or diminished in hopes of creating race-neutral practices.

Promising Practices for Being a Student of the Community

Listening and Learning. Scholars agree that an important culturally responsive leadership practice is to listen and learn from Latina/o/x communities. Asset-based approaches to this are critical. Gardiner and Enomoto (2006) found that principals' willingness to learn about multicultural issues oriented them toward being better situated to serve diverse students. *Asset-based* approaches include drawing on "*funds of knowledge* of Latina/o/x communities" which is based on the assumption that "people are competent, they have knowledge, and their life experiences have given them that knowledge" (González et al., 2005, pp. ix–x). Further, school leaders can learn from their communities. *Community cultural wealth* is connected to this. Changing beliefs and assumptions about Latina/o/x families is an important first step, which can take place through reflection and discussion with families and colleagues.

Other asset-based approaches for engaging Latina/o/x communities include community-based equity audits (Green, 2017) and radical care. Green (2017) describes *community-based equity audits* as an "instrument, strategy, process, and approach to guide educational leaders in supporting equitable school-community outcomes" (p. 5). Education leaders work alongside community members and engage in inquiry and other experiences together. A key phase is the disruption of deficit views about the community. *Radical care* is a framework in which school leaders develop antiracism and authentic relationships. Leaders believe that teachers and students are capable of excellence. Leaders also and leverage their power strategically (Rivera-McCutchen, 2021).

Social Justice Advocacy

Enrique spoke about the importance of redesigning inequitable school systems. He declared:

> This idea that we're in this business to save as many lives as possible is the way I see it. I told someone the other day that our system wasn't designed for the kids that we serve. Our system was never designed for low income, like Latinx, African American kids to make it. And so our job is to redesign the system, so that these kids do have an opportunity. And that's what I enjoy doing. So whenever a kid that wasn't supposed to make it makes it, I get happy. Because I often remind people, don't use me as a reason why the system works. I often refer to myself as a human outlier. I'm one of fifty [others] that didn't make it. And so maybe what we need to do is make it so that these kids do make it by redesigning that system.

All school leaders should develop their capacity for social justice advocacy with the same level of tenacity as their Latina/o/x counterparts. Although the motivation and insight into the lived experiences of Latina/o/x families will be different because non-Latina/o/x leaders will not have shared experiences, a commitment to equity based on a belief that Latina/o/x families are capable of academic success is essential. Two important aspects of social justice advocacy for Latina/o/x communities are *upholding bilingualism* and *redesigning inequitable systems*. Martina offered ways to promote bilingualism in schools, starting with administrators becoming bi- or multilingual themselves. She suggested:

> whenever you can, obviously trying to increase your capacity in the building of having bilingual people. And then for principals themselves, it's never, ever too late to want to learn the language. So, it goes a long way for people who start taking classes. Finding ways to become fully bilingual, maybe that's the long-term goal, but even having a few tools of learning a few languages.

As evidence of Martina's lifelong interest and commitment to multilingualism, she added, "Like in my case now, I'm learning Arabic. One, because I believe that Arabic is going to be a big language in the US in the next decade. Initially in my field, you want to know even some phrases."

Finally, to redesign inequitable school systems, "[l]eaders need a deep understanding of their school content to provide successful education for Latinos" and to assess ways in which racism is "embedded within the school context" (González, 2010, p. 486). Again, we reiterate that a dangerous form of racism is the maintenance of low expectations for Latina/o/x students (McCutchen, 2021).

CONCLUSION

As we stated in the introduction, we draw upon Rodríguez et al.'s (2016) assertion that preparing leaders from an Applied Critical Leadership framework "to serve and empower Latino communities and improve access and equity in schools and educational systems overall is paramount to the concept of Latino Educational Leadership" (p. 148). The *testimonios* of eight Latina/o/x leaders provide insight into research-based practices associated with Latina/o/x social justice leaders. Through their stories, we identified equity-oriented mindsets and practices that emanated from a commitment to eliminate deficit beliefs. Non-Latina/o/x leaders can actualize these mindsets and practices, too.

It is evident that school leaders chronicled here and in extant research, draw upon their community cultural wealth to frame their understanding of social justice advocacy. The leaders also shared how they engage in culturally responsive advocacy, a related concept (Khalifa et al., 2016). An important line of inquiry ought to be how advocacy practices of Latina/o/x leaders create change in organizational decision-making. Additionally, as research about Latina/o/x school leaders continues, it is important to ask how an understanding of their community cultural wealth informs P-12 school practice. How do, or can, the practices of Latina/o/x administrators who operate from their cultural perspectives create change in the fabric of school institutions? It is also important to investigate the ways in which Latino Educational Leadership shifts organizational responsibility toward improving the educational lives of Latina/o/x students, families, and communities. Finally, to further explore the concept of engraving, an essential question researchers, practitioners, and those preparing school leaders should ponder is: How do their P-12 school districts leverage, value, or incorporate the community cultural wealth of Latina/o/x school leaders?

Afterword

Most of the leaders chronicled in this book have moved to new positions and in some cases new cities since our interviews.

Antonio is still an author and consultant.

Cecilia remains a director of bilingual education.

George was appointed a central office administration position and is now an assistant superintendent in a new city and school district.

Martha remains a principal at the same elementary school.

Martina held a couple of different administrative positions in different cities. She is now an assistant superintendent of teaching and learning in a new city and school district.

Sonia is a superintendent in a new city and school district.

Velma is still a principal at the same school.

References

Alemán, E., Jr. (2009). Through the prism of critical race theory: Niceness and Latina/o leadership in the politics of education. *Journal of Latinos and Education, 8*(4), 290–311.

Almager, I. L., Méndez-Morse, S., & Murakami, E. (2018). Voices of Texas Latina school leaders. In C. Rodríguez, M. A. Martinez, & F. Valle (Eds.), *Latino educational leadership: Serving Latino communities and preparing Latinx leaders across the P-20 pipeline* (pp. 25–37). Information Age Publishing, Inc.

Aragon, A. (2017). Achieving Latina students: Aspirational counterstories and critical reflections on parental community cultural wealth. *Journal of Latinos and Education, 17*(4), 373–385. http://dx.doi.org/10.1080/15348431.2017.1355804

Avalos, M., & Salgados, Y. (2016). Legacy of hope: Latinas overcoming barriers to success. *National Forum of Educational Administration & Supervision Journal, 34*(4), 24–31.

Banks, J. A. (1993). Multicultural education: Historical development, dimensions, and practice. *Review of Research in Education, 19*, 3–49.

Bell, D. A., Jr. (1980). *Brown v. Board of Education* and the interest-convergence dilemma. *Harvard Law Review, 93*(3), 518–533. https://www.jstor.org/stable/1340546

Bernal, D. D. (2002). Critical race theory, Latino critical theory, and critical raced-gendered epistemologies: Recognizing students of color as holders and creators of knowledge. *Qualitative Inquiry, 8*(1), 105–126.

Brayboy, B. M. J. (2006). Toward a tribal critical race theory in education. *The Urban Review, 37*(5), 425–446. https:doi.org/10.1007/s11256-005-0018-y

Byrne-Jiménez, M., & Garcia, W. (2021). *Un Cafecito:* Three Afro-Latina leaders speak their truth. In M. A. Martínez & S. Méndez-Morse (Eds.), *Latinas leading schools* (pp. 65–81). Information Age Publishing, Inc.

Cambron-McCabe, N., & McCarthy, M. (2005). Educating school leaders for social justice. *Educational Policy, 19*(4), 201–222.

Ceja, M. (2004). Chicana college aspirations and the role of parents: Developing educational resiliency. *Journal of Hispanic Higher Education, 3*(4), 338–362. https://doi.org/10.1177/1538192704268428

Collins, P. H. (1990). *Black feminist thought: Knowledge, consciousness, and the politics of empowerment.* Routledge.

Cooper Stein, K., Wright, J., Gil, E., Miness, A., & Ginanto, D. (2018). Examining Latina/o students' experiences of injustices: LatCrit insights from a Texas high school. *Journal of Latinos and Education, 17*(2), 103–120. https://doi.org/10.1080/15348431.2017.1282367

Crawford, E. R., & Fuller, E. J. (2017). A dream attained or deferred? Examination of production and placement of Latino administrators. *Urban Education, 52*(10), 1167–1203. https://doi.org/10.1177/0042085915602537

Crenshaw, K. (1991). Mapping the margins: Intersectionality, identity politics, and violence against women of color. *Stanford Law Review, 43*(6), 1241–1299. https://www.jstor.org/stable/1229039

Dantley, M. E., & Tillman, L. (2010). Social justice and moral transformative leadership. In C. Marshall & M. Oliva (Eds.), *Leadership for social justice* (2nd ed., pp. 19–34). Allyn & Bacon.

Davila, E. R., & Aviles de Bradley, A. (2010). Examining education for Latinas/os in Chicago: A CRT/LatCrit approach. *Educational Foundations, 24*, 39–58.

Delgado, R. (1984). The imperial scholar: Reflections on a review of civil rights literature. *University of Pennsylvania Law Review, 132*, 561–578.

Delgado, R. (1989). Storytelling for oppositionists and others: A plea for narrative. *Michigan Law Review, 87*(8), 2411–2441. https://www.jstor.org/stable/1289308

Delgado, R., & Stefancic, J. (2017). *Critical race theory: An introduction* (3rd ed.). New York University Press.

DeMatthews, D., Izquierdo, E., & Knight, D. S. (2017). Righting past wrongs: A superintendent's social justice leadership for dual language education along the U.S.-Mexico border. *Education Policy Analysis Archives, 25*(1), 1–29. http://dx.doi.org/10.14507/epaa.25.2436

DeMatthews, D. E., Edwards, D. B., Jr., & Rincones, R. (2016). Social justice leadership and family engagement: A successful case from Ciudad Juárez, Mexico. *Educational Administration Quarterly, 52*(5), 754–792. https://doi.org/10.1177/0013161X16664006

DeNicolo, C. P., González, M., Morales, S., & Romaní, L. (2015). Teaching through testimonio: Accessing community cultural wealth in school. *Journal of Latinos and Education, 14*, 228–243. http://dx.doi.org/10.1080/15348431.2014.1000541

Duncheon, J. C. (2018). "You have to be able to adjust your own self": Latinx students' transitions into college from a low-performing urban high school. *Journal of Latinos and Education, 17*(4), 358–372. https://doi.org/10.1080/15348431.2017.1355248

Fernandez, R., Bustamante, R. M., Combs, J. P., & Martinez-Garcia, C. (2015). Career experiences of Latino/a secondary principals in suburban school districts. *International Journal of Educational Leadership Preparation, 10*(1), 60–76.

Freeman, A. D. (1978). Legitimizing racial discrimination through antidiscrimination law: A critical review of Supreme Court doctrine. *Minnesota Law Review, 62*, 1049–1119.

Furman, G. (2012). Social justice leadership as praxis: Developing capacities through preparation programs. *Educational Administration Quarterly, 48*(2), 191–229. https://doi.org/10.1177/0013161X11427394

Galindo, C. L. (2021). Taking an equity lens: Reconceptualizing research on Latinx students' schooling experiences and educational outcomes. *The Annals of the American Academy of Political and Social Science, 696*(1), 106–127. https://doi.org/10.1177/00027162211043770

Gándara, P. C., & Aldana, U. S. (2014). Who's segregated now? Latinos, language, and the future of integrated schools. *Educational Administration Quarterly, 50*(5), 735–748. https://doi.org/10.1177/0013161X14549957

Gardiner, M. E., & Enomoto, E. (2006). Urban school principals and their role as multicultural leaders. *Urban Education, 41*, 560–584. https://doi.org/10.1177/0042085906294504

Gay, G. (2010). *Culturally responsive teaching: Theory, research, and practice* (2nd ed.). Teachers College Press.

Gay, G. Gil, E. (2021). *From community schools to schools to community: A Latina educational leader's social justice trajectory*. In M. A. Martinez & S. Méndez-Morse (Eds.), Latinas leading schools (pp. 83–96). Information Age Publishing, Inc.

Gil, E. (2021). *From community schools to schools to community: A Latina educational leader's social justice trajectory*. In M. A. Martinez & S. Méndez-Morse (Eds.), Latinas leading schools (pp. 83–96). Information Age Publishing, Inc.

González, M. L. (2010). The critical role of all educators in the school success of Latino children. *Leadership and Policy in Schools, 9*, 479–494. https://doi.org/10.1080/15700763.2010.493635

González, N., Moll, L. C., & Amanti, C. (Eds.). (2005). *Funds of knowledge: Theorizing practices in households, communities, and classrooms*. Routledge.

Green, T. L. (2017). Community-based equity audits: A practical approach for educational leaders to support equitable community-school improvements. *Educational Administration Quarterly, 53*(1), 3–39. http://dx.doi.org/10.1177/0013161X16672513

Grice, A. W., & Parker, L. (2018). Educational cultural negotiators for students of color: A descriptive study of racial advocacy leaders. *Race Ethnicity and Education, 21*(1), 45–62. https://doi.org/10.1080/13613324.2017.1294565

Guzmán, B. L., Kouyoumdjian, C., Medrano, J. A., & Bernal, I. (2021). Community cultural wealth and immigrant Latino parents. *Journal of Latinos and Education, 20*(1), 78–92. https://doi.org/10.1080/15348431.2018.1541801

Harris, A. P. (1994). Foreword: The jurisprudence of reconstruction. *California Law Review, 82*(4), 741–785.

Hayes, D., Blake, J. J., Darensbourg, A., & Castillo, L. G. (2015). Examining the academic achievement of Latino adolescents: The role of parent and peer beliefs and behaviors. *Journal of Early Adolescence, 35*(2), 141–161.

Hernandez, F., & Murakami, E. (2016a). *Brown-eyed leaders of the sun: A portrait of Latina/o educational leaders*. Information Age Publishing, Inc.

Hernandez, F., & Murakami, E. (2016b). Counterstories about leadership: A Latina school principal's experience from a less documented view in an urban school context. *Education Sciences, 6*(6), 1–16. http://dx.doi.org/10.3390/educsci6010006

Hernandez, F., Murakami, E. T., & Cerecer, P. Q. (2014). A Latina principal leading for social justice: Influences of racial and gender identity. *Journal of School Leadership, 24*, 568–598.

Hernández-Truyol, B. E., Harris, A., & Valdés, F. (2006). Beyond the first decade: A forward-lookig history of LatCrit theory, community, and praxis. *La Raza Law Journal, 17*, 169–216.

Howard, T. C. (2010). *Why race and culture matter in schools: Closing the achievement gap in America's classrooms.* Teachers College Press.

Iftikar, J. S., & Museus, S. D. (2019). On the utility of Asian critical (AsianCrit) theory in the field of education. *International Journal of Qualitative Studies in Education, 31*(10), 935–949. https://doi.org/10.1080/09518398.2018.1522008

Kemp-Graham, K. Y. (2015). Missed opportunities: Preparing aspiring school leaders for bold social justice school leadership needed for 21st century schools. *NCPEA International Journal of Educational Leadership Preparation, 10*(21), 99–129.

Khalifa, M. A., Gooden, M. A., & Davis, J. E. (2016). Culturally responsive school leadership: A synthesis of the literature. *Review of Educational Research, 86*(4), 1272–1311. https://doi.org/10.3102/0034654316630383

Kouyoumdjian, C., Guzmán, B. L., Garcia, N. M., & Talavera-Bustillos, V. (2017). A community cultural wealth examination of sources of support and challenges among Latino first- and second-generation college students at a Hispanic serving institution. *Journal of Hispanic Higher Education, 16*(1), 61–76. https://doi.org/10.1177/1538192715619995

Ladson-Billings, G. (2009). *The dreamkeepers: Successful teachers of African American children* (2nd ed.). Jossey-Bass.

Ladson-Billings, G. (2021). Critical race theory – What it is not! In M. Lynn & A. D. Dixson (Eds.), *Handbook of critical race theory in education* (2nd ed., pp. 32–43). Routledge.

Ladson-Billings, G., & Tate, W. F. (1995). Toward a critical race theory of education. *Teachers College Record, 97*(1), 47–68.

Lewis, M. M., & Kern, S. (2018). Using education law as a tool to empower social justice leaders to promote LGBTQ inclusion. *Educational Administration Quarterly.* Advance online publication. https://doi.org/10.1177/0013161X18769045

Liou, D. D., Antrop-González, R., & Cooper, R. (2009). Unveiling the promise of community cultural wealth to sustaining Latina/o students' college-going information networks. *Educational Studies, 45*, 534–555. https://doi.org/10.1080/00131940903311347

Lombardi, J. D. (2016, June 14). The deficit model is harming your students. *Edutopia.* https://www.edutopia.org/blog/deficit-model-is-harming-students-janice-lombardi

Lowery, K., & Romero-Johnson, S. (2018). Advocacy in practice: Factors that influence Latinx school leaders' advocacy for increasing educational access for Latinx students and families. In C. Rodríguez, M. A. Martinez, & F. Valle (Eds.), *Latino educational leadership: Serving Latino communities and preparing Latinx leaders across the P-20 pipeline.* Information Age Publishing, Inc.

Luna, N. A., & Martinez, M. (2013). A qualitative study using community cultural wealth to understand the educational experiences of Latino college students. *Journal of Praxis in Multicultural Education, 7*(1), 1–18. http://digitalscholarship.unlv.edu/jpme/vol7/iss1/2

Magdaleno, K. R. (2006). Mentoring Latino school leaders. *Leadership, 36*(1), 12–14.

Marbley, A. F., Malott, K. M., Flaherty, A., & Helyne, F. (2011). Three issues, three approaches, three calls to action: Multicultural social justice in the schools. *Journal for Social Action in Counseling and Psychology, 3*(1), 59–73.

Martin-Beltrán, M., Montoya-Ávila, A., García, A. A., & Canales, N. (2018). "Do you want to tell your own narrative?": How one teacher and her students engage in resistance by leveraging community cultural wealth. *Association of Mexican American Educators Journal, 12*(3), 97–121.

Martinez, M. A., Marquez, J., Cantú, Y., & Rocha, P. A. (2016). *Ternura y tenacidad: Testimonios* of Latina school leaders. *Association of Mexican American Educators (AMAE) Journal, 10*(3), 11–29.

Martinez, M. A., & Méndez-Morse, S. (Eds.). (2021). *Latinas leading schools*. Information Age Publishing, Inc.

Martinez, M. A., Rivera, M., & Marquez, J. (2020). Learning from the experiences and development of Latina school leaders. *Educational Administration Quarterly, 56*(3), 472–498. https://doi.org/10.1177/0013161X19866491

McCarther, S. M., Davis, D. M., Nilsson, J., Marszalek, J , & Barber, C. (2012). Social justice advocacy competency: A step on the journey to develop an analytic instrument to pinpoint development and build capacity in 21st century school leaders. *National Forum of Applied Educational Research Journal, 26*(1&2), 94–100.

McCarty, T. L., & Lee, T. S. (2014). Critical culturally sustaining/revitalizing pedagogy and indigenous education sovereignty. *Harvard Educational Review, 84*(1), 101–124. https://doi.org/10.17763/haer.84.1.q83746nl5pj34216

McNair, D. E. (2014). A tap on the shoulder: External influences as catalysts for professional change. *Community College Journal of Research and Practice, 38*(2–3), 184–193. https://doi.org/10.1080/10668926.2014.851963

Menchaca, V. D., Mills, S. J., & Leo, F. (2017). Latina school leadership: Breaking the mold and rising to the top. *Journal of Women in Educational Leadership*. Advance online publication. https://doi.org/10.13014/K2SF2TC9

Méndez-Morse, S. (2000). Claiming forgotten leadership. *Urban Education, 35*(5), 584–596.

Méndez-Morse, S. (2004). Constructing mentors: Latina educational leaders' role models and mentors. *Educational Administration Quarterly, 40*(4), 561–590. https://doi.org/10.1177/0013161X04267112

Méndez-Morse, S., & Martinez, M. A. (2021). Why Latina school leaders? An introduction to this needed book. In M. A. Martínez & S. Méndez-Morse (Eds.), *Latinas leading schools* (pp. xi–xxiv). Information Age Publishing, Inc.

Mora, G. C., Perez, R., & Vargas, N. (2022). Who identifies as "Latinx"? The generational politics of ethnoracial labels. *Social Forces, 100*(3), 1170–1194. https://doi.org/10.1093/sf/soab011

Murakami, E., Hernandez, F., Valle, F., & Almager, I. (2018). Latina/o school administrators and the intersectionality of professional identity and race. *SAGE Open, 8*(2), 1–16. https://doi.org/10.1177/2158244018776045

Murakami, E. T., Hernandez, F., Mendez-Morse, S., & Byrne-Jimenez, M. (2016). Latina/o school principals: Identity, leadership and advocacy. *International Journal of Leadership in Education, 19*(3), 280–299. http://dx.doi.org/10.1080/13603124.2015.1025854

National Center for Education Statistics. (2021a). *Public high school graduation rates*. https://nces.ed.gov/programs/coe/indicator/coi

National Center for Education Statistics. (2022b). *Racial/ethnic enrollment in public schools*. https://nces.ed.gov/programs/coe/indicator/cge

National Center for Education Statistics. (2022c, May 2022). *Status dropout rates*. https://nces.ed.gov/programs/coe/indicator/coj

Nieto, S. (2017). Re-imagining multicultural education: New visions, new possibilities. *Multicultural Education Review, 1*, 1–10. http://dx.doi.org/10.1080/2005615X.2016.1276671

Niño, J. M. (2018). Latino superintendent leadership: A case of Texas district leaders. In C. Rodríguez, M. A. Martinez, & F. Valle (Eds.), *Latino educational leadership: Serving Latino communities and preparing latinx leaders across the P-20 pipeline* (pp. 57–75). Information Age Publishing, Inc.

Orfield, G., Ee, J., Frankenberg, E., & Siegel-Hawley, G. (2016). *Brown at 62: School segregation by race, poverty and state*. Civil Rights Project/*Proyecto Derechos Civiles*, UCLA.

Ormand, C. (2019, May 16). *SAGE musings: Shifting from deficit thinking to asset thinking*. SAGE 2YC: 2YC Faculty as Agents of Change. https://serc.carleton.edu/sage2yc/musings/deficit_thinking.html

Ortiz, F. I. (2001). Using social capital in interpreting the careers of three Latina superintendents. *Educational Administration Quarterly, 37*(1), 58–85.

Ortiz, F.Owens, T. M., & Harris, S. L. (2021). *Latinas overcoming challenges to become school leaders*. In M. A. Martinez & S. Méndez-Morse (Eds.), Latinas leading schools (pp.137–158). Information Age Publishing, Inc.

Owens, T. M., & Harris, S. L. (2021). *Latinas overcoming challenges to become school leaders*. In M. A. Martinez & S. Méndez-Morse (Eds.), Latinas leading schools (pp.137–158). Information Age Publishing, Inc.

Paris, D., & Alim, H. S. (2014). What are we seeking to sustain through culturally sustaining pedagogy? A loving critique forward. *Harvard Educational Review, 84*(1), 85–100. https://doi.org/10.17763/haer.84.1.982l873k2ht16m77

Pérez, D., II. (2017). In pursuit of success; Latino male college students excercising academic determination and community cultural wealth. *Journal of College Student Development, 58*(2), 123–140. https://doi.org/10.1353/csd.2017.0011

Pounder, D., Reitzug, U., & Young, M. (2005). Preparing school leaders for school improvement, social justice, and community. *Yearbook of the National Society for the Study of Education, 101*(1), 261–288. https://doi.org/10.111/j.1744-7984.2002.tb00012.x

Pstross, M., Rodriguez, A., Knopf, R. C., & Paris, C. M. (2016). Empowering Latino parents to transform the education of their children. *Education and Urban Society, 48*(7), 650–671. https://doi.org/10.1177/0013124514541464

Renkly, S., & Bertolini, K. (2018). Shifting the paradigm from deficit oriented schools to asset based models: Why leaders need to promote an asset orientation in our schools. *Empowering Research for Educators, 2*(1), 23–27. https://openprairie.sdstate.edu/ere/vol2/iss1/4

Rivera-McCutchen, R. L. (2021). "We don't got time for grumbling": Toward an ethic of radical care in urban school leadership. *Educational Administration Quarterly, 57*(2), 257–289. https://doi.org/10.1177/0013161X20925892

Rodela, K., Rodriguez-Mojica, C., & Cochrun, A. (2019). "You guys are bilingual aren't you?": Latinx educational leadership pathways in the new Latinx diaspora. *International Journal of Leadership in Education*. Advance online publication. https://doi.org/10.1080/13603124.2019.1566577

Rodela, K. C., & Rodriguez-Mojica, C. (2019). Equity leadership informed by community cultural wealth: Counterstories of Latinx school administrators. *Educational Administration Quarterly*. Advance online publication. https://doi.org/10.1177/0013161X19847513

Rodríguez, C., Martinez, M. A., & Valle, F. (2016). Latino educational leadership across the pipeline: For Latino communities and Latina/o leaders. *Journal of Hispanic Higher Education*, *15*(2), 136–153. https://doi.org/10.1177/1538192715612914

Rodríguez, C., Martinez, M. A., & Valle, F. (Eds.). (2018). *Latino educational leadership: Serving Latino communities and preparing Latinx leaders across the P-20 pipeline*. Information Age Publishing, Inc.

Rodriguez, H., Mireles-Rios, R., & Conley, S. (2018). Perceptions of Latina K-12 leaders' experiences with mentorship and career advancement. *CLEARvoz Journal*, *4*(2), 1–16.

Rolón-Dow, R., & Davison, A. (2020). Theorizing racial microaffirmations: A critical race/LatCrit approach. *Race Ethnicity and Education*, *24*(2), 245–261. https://doi.org/10.1080/13613324.2020.1798381

Saldaña, J. (2009). *The coding manual for qualitative researchers*. Sage Publications Ltd.

Sampson, C. (2019). (Im)possibilities of Latinx school board members' educational leadership toward equity. *Educational Administration Quarterly*, *55*(2), 296–327. https://doi.org/10.1177/0013161X18799482

San Miguel, G., Jr. (2011). Embracing *Latinidad*: Beyond nationalism in the history of education. *Journal of Latinos and Education*, *10*(1), 3–22. https://doi.org/10.1080/15348431.2011.531655

Sanchez, J., Thornton, B., & Usinger, J. (2008). Promoting diversity within public education leadership. *International Journal of Educational Leadership Preparation*, *3*(3), 1–10. https://files.eric.ed.gov/fulltext/EJ1067212.pdf

Santamaría, L. J. (2014). Critical change for the greater good: Multicultural perceptions in educational leadership toward social justice and equity. *Educational Administration Quarterly*, *50*(3), 347–391. https://doi.org/10.1177/0013161X13505287

Santamaría, L. J., & Santamaría, A. P. (2012). *Applied critical leadership in education: Choosing change*. Routledge.

Santamaría, L. J., & Santamaría, A. P. (2015). Counteracting educational injustice with applied critical leadership: Culturally responsive practices promoting sustainable change. *International Journal of Multicultural Education*, *17*(1), 22–41. https://doi.org/10.18251/ijme.v17i1.1013

Santamaría, L. J., Santamaría, A. P., & Dam, L. I. (2014). Applied critical leadership through Latino/a lenses: An alternative approach to educational leadership. *International Journal of Education for Social Justice*, *3*(2), 161–180.

Shaked, H. (2020). Social justice leadership, instructional leadership, and the goals of schooling. *International Journal of Educational Management*, *34*(1), 81–95. https://doi.org/10.1108/IJEM-01-2019-0018

Solórzano, D. G. (1998). Critical race theory, race and gender microaggressions, and the experience of Chicana and Chicano scholars. *International Journal of Qualitative Studies in Education, 11*, 121–136. https://doi.org/10.1080/095183998236926

Solórzano & Bernal (2001): Solórzano, D. G., & Yosso, T. J. (2000). *Toward a critical race theory of Chicana and Chicano education*. In C. Tejeda, C. Martinez, & Z. Leonardo (Eds.), Charting new terrains of Chicana(o)/Latina(o) education (pp. 35–65). Hampton Press, Inc.

Solórzano, D. G., & Bernal, D. D. (2001). Examining transformational resistance through a critical race and Latcrit theory framework: Chicana and Chicano students in an urban context. *Urban Education, 36*(3), 308–342. https://doi.org/10.1177/0042085901363002

Solórzano, D. G., & Yosso, T. J. (2001). Critical race and LatCrit theory and method: Counter-storytelling. *International Journal of Qualitative Studies in Education, 14*(4), 471–495. https://doi.org/10.1080/09518390110063365

Solórzano, D. G., & Yosso, T. J. (2002). Critical race methodology: Counter-storytelling as an analytical framework for education research. *Qualitative Inquiry, 8*(1), 23–44.

Theoharis, G. (2007). Social justice educational leaders and resistance: Toward a theory of social justice leadership. *Educational Administration Quarterly, 43*, 221–258. https://doi.org/10.1177/0013161X06293717

Tooms, A. (2007). An international effort to build leadership capacity: Insights from the first cohort of educational administration at the College of the Bahamas. *Journal of Research on Leadership Education, 2*(2), 1–41.

U.S. Department of Labor. (2022). Employed persons by detailed occupation, sex, race, and Hispanic or Latino ethnicity. Household data annual averages. https://www.bls.gov/cps/cpsaat11.pdf

Valencia, R. R. (2010). *Dismantling contemporary deficit thinking: Educational thought and practice*. Routledge.

Vega, D., Moore, J. L., & Miranda, A. H. (2015). In their own words: Perceived barriers to achievement by African American and Latino high school students. *American Secondary Education, 43*(3), 36–59.

Vidal-Ortiz, S., & Martínez, J. (2018). Latinx thoughts: Latinidad with an X. *Latino Studies, 16*(3), 384–395. https://doi.org/10.1057/s41276-018-0137-8

Villegas, A. M., & Lucas, T. (2002). Preparing culturally responsive teachers: Rethinking the curriculum. *Journal of Teacher Education, 53*(1), 20–32.

West, C. (1995). Foreward. In K. Crenshaw, N. Gotanda, G. Peller, & K. Thomas (Eds.), *Critical race theory: The key writings that formed the movement* (pp. xi–xii). The New Press.

Williams, P. J. (1991). *The alchemy of race and rights*. Harvard University Press.

Yosso, T. (2005). Whose culture has capital? A critical race theory discussion of community cultural wealth. *Race Ethnicity and Education, 8*(1), 69–91. https://doi.org/10.1080/1361332052000341006

Yosso, T. J., Villalpando, O., Bernal, D. D., & Solórzano, D. G. (2001). Critical race theory in Chicana/o education. National Association for Chicana and Chicano Studies Annual Conference Paper 9.

Index

advocacy, 2, 18, 22, 40, 80, 89; explanation, 28–30; power to enact and influence, 58–59; self-advocacy, 82. *See also* social justice, advocacy

asset(s), 4, 6, 8, 9, 11, 23, 25, 27, 32, 38, 51, 52, 67, 69, 80, 81, 86; cultural, 9

asset-based, 8, 82, 87; family and community engagement, 81–82; inquiry, 82; perspective, 11, 46, 87; thinking, 5–7, 8; understanding, 8, 23. *See also* deficit(s), differences between deficit- and asset-based thinking

assumptions, 6, 7, 21, 45, 54, 62, 67, 71, 87

bilingualism, 2, 27, 33, 52, 53, 67, 69, 76, 77, 80–81, 86, 88. *See also* capital, linguistic

capital, 24, 28, 41, 80; aspirational, 23, 41–45, 80; cultural, 23; familial, 23, 24–25, 41, 45–47, 80; linguistic, 23, 27, 51–53, 57, 58, 59, 67, 69, 77, 80; navigational, 23, 25; resistant, 23; social, 23, 72

community cultural wealth, 5, 14, 17, 22, 31, 33, 34, 40, 77, 80, 83, 84, 85, 87; also cultural wealth, 5, 8, 9, 23, 45, 80; explanation of Yosso's (2005) article, 23; of school leaders, 41–54, 89; summary of research, 23–27;

critical race theory, 17, 23, 31, 77, 83, 84; counternarratives, 21–22, 40; counter-stories, 21; in education, 19; explanation of, 18–19; Latino Critical Race Theory (LatCrit), 19–21, 31, 77, 83

culturally responsive school leadership, 5, 8, 17, 22, 31, 77, 83; explanation, 30

deficit(s), 21, 23, 24, 30, 43, 54, 68, 79, 81, 88, 89; anti-deficit-based thinking, 77, -based, 5, 6, 8; differences between deficit- and asset-based thinking, 5–7; dismantle, 83; -laden, 6, 80; perspectives, 8; thinking, 6, 9, 18, 31, 56, 67, 68, 75, 83; views, 48, 69, 88

engraving, 9, 14, 32, 85–89; questions for, 54, 62, 76

equity, 5, 7, 9, 12, 24, 26, 28, 30, 31, 33, 58, 70, 71, 75, 82, 88, 89; community-based equity audits, 87; equity-minded, 1; equity-oriented, 4

high expectations, 7, 42, 56–57, 59,
    66–67, 75, 79, 80; high academic
    expectations, 2, 24–25, 33,
    66–67, 75, 80. *See also* capital,
    aspirational

identity/identities, 13, 17, 20, 24,
    26, 27, 29, 31, 47, 49, 52, 64,
    65, 80, 87; cultural, 27, 46, 52,
    53, 58, 63; ethnic, 2, 52, 75;
    ethnoracial labels, 12; gender, 27;
    Latinidad (Latino identity), 77–79;
    leadership, 75; professional, 29;
    racial, 25, 80
immigration, 20, 27, 58, 69, 80; anti-
    immigration, 33; experience, 38,
    47–51, 54, 72; immigrant(s), 35, 37,
    38, 42, 44, 45, 46, 57, 67, 81
inequity/inequities, 1, 7, 19, 30, 32, 70;
    dismantling, 1

Latina/o/x Educational Leadership, 5,
    15, 17, 22, 77–84; engraving, 85–89;
    explanation of, 31–33
lived experiences, vii, 3, 4, 5, 8, 10, 12,
    17, 19, 20, 21, 28, 31, 32, 40, 41, 53,
    80, 88

mentoring, 25, 26, 62; lack of for
    Latina administrators, 26; same race
    mentoring, 26, 86; "tap(ping) on the
    shoulder," 55–56, 59, 62, 86
multilingual(ism), 2, 23, 35, 38, 53,
    68–69, 70, 88

relationships, 7, 21, 25, 88; mentoring,
    26; with staff, 70; with students,
    families, parents, and community, 1,
    2, 27, 33, 69, 70, 71, 82

social justice: advocacy, 8, 14, 28, 30,
    33, 63–76, 77, 82, 83–84, 87, 88, 89;
    leadership, 12, 14, 17, 22, 24, 27, 28,
    77, 83, 84
strengths, 2, 4, 5, 6, 7, 24, 53, 56,
    80, 86; strength-based, 5. *See also*
    asset(s); asset-based

testimonio(s), 14, 21, 24, 25, 33, 43, 45,
    47, 50, 52, 53, 67, 71, 75, 77, 80, 84,
    89; explanation of, 22

Yosso, Tara: community cultural wealth,
    5, 17, 23, 41, 42, 45, 47, 53, 80, 83;
    critical race theory, 18, 19, 21, 83

About the Authors

Kendra Lowery, PhD, is associate dean for Equity and Engagement and associate professor of educational leadership in Teachers College at Ball State University. She was a teacher and administrator in P-12 schools before entering higher education. Kendra's research agenda includes leadership practices that promote social justice with attention to the experiences of Black and Latina/o/x school leaders, diversity and inclusion in organizational decision-making, cross-racial dialogues, and arts-based research.

Dr. Silvia Romero-Johnson is an educational leader in the field of K-12 education. She started her career as a paraprofessional working as liaison, interpreter, and translator for Spanish-speaking students and families. She became a bilingual mathematics teacher in bilingual programs. She then became a principal for a whole school dual language education community school. She has been serving in cabinet level administrative positions in urban and suburban districts. She is a coauthor of the book *Advancing Equity in Dual Language Education: A Guide for Leaders*. Her passion is to provide leadership for continuous improvement for leadership teams to embrace culturally and linguistically sustaining and inclusive instruction.

Ingram Content Group UK Ltd.
Milton Keynes UK
UKHW040352020523
421006UK00025B/8

9 781793 615268